Other photo-bios of music stars
available from Jove/HBJ

# FRAMPTON!

# TRAVOLTA!

## WHERE DOES DOLLY GO FROM HERE?

For someone with her talent, her ambition and her remarkable physical presence, the possibilities are almost limitless. She could be the biggest woman star in the music business, ever.

She could be the new Elvis Presley.

The parallels are all there. Like Elvis, she has burst out of Southern genre music and onto the nationwide scene, into the big time, leaving a hole in the fabric of conventional expectations so wide that others are following.

# DOLLY PARTON

## A PHOTO-BIO

### OTIS JAMES

A JOVE/HBJ BOOK

## PHOTO CREDITS

Front cover: © David Gahr 1977; Back cover © David Gahr 1977

© Richard E. Aaron, Pp. 113, 148-149, 151, 154b

© Jody Caravaglia 1978, Pp. 100, 101, 170

Country Music Foundation, Pp. 26, 27, 30, 55t, 55b

Frank Edwards/Pictorial Parade, Inc., P. 24

Carl Fleischhauer, Pp. 32t, 38, 48, 49, 73t

© David Gahr, Pp. 2, 4, 8, 9, 14, 20-21, 36-37, 68, 69, 80, 83,
84-85, 96, 97, 114, 115, 122, 123, 129t, 129b, 156, 157, 160t, 160b,
161t, 161b, 162, 163, 164, 165, 168-169, 173t, 173b, 174, 176,
177, 180

© Tom Hill Photography 1978, Pp. 140, 141, 144, 145t, 145b

Henry Horenstein, Pp. 43, 75

© Slick Lawson 1978/Camera 5, Inc., Pp. 12-13, 32b, 56, 57, 78,
104-105, 126-127, 128, 130, 136-137

John Lee, Pp. 16, 17, 19, 35, 90-91, 103, 106, 108, 110-111

Les Leverett, Pp. 31, 40, 41, 61, 62-63, 66, 73b, 76-77, 94

© Allan Tannenbaum, Pp. 133, 134, 152, 154t

Sam Trent, Pp. 45, 89, 93

United Press International Photos Pp. 22

World Wide Photos, Pp. 147

Charlene Zlotnik Photography, Pp. 118, 119, 120, 172

Printed in the United States of America
Library of Congress Catalog Card Number: 78-56222
First Jove/HBJ edition published February 1979

Jove/HBJ books are published by Jove Publications, Inc.
(Harcourt Brace Jovanovich) 757 Third Avenue, New York,
N.Y. 10017

**DOLLY PARTON**

A
PHOTO
BIO

1

The first question you're probably asking yourself is, "How long can he go without mentioning Dolly Parton's physical attributes?" Well, let's end the suspense right at the outset. Dolly Parton is one of the most striking and astonishing beauties of our time, a triumph of nature wedded to a triumph of artifice, an anachronism, and, perhaps, the new sex symbol of the seventies. Her face is round and dimpled, and framed in a platinum blonde wig that looks like a bubbling fountain caught in the glinting light of a clear blue morning by a high-speed camera. It foams, roils, rolls and tumbles in wild profusion, and perfect, man-made symmetry. Her blue eyes are clear, direct and compelling as beacons, and surrounded by long false lashes that point the way to them like signposts on a Tennessee highway. Her smile would light up a dark room with just the candlepower of her inner warmth; but for good measure, it is encased in lipstick that almost glows in the dark.

And the rest of her ... well, yes. Breathtaking.

# DOLLY PARTON

Magnificent. Gravity defying. If the phrase hour-glass figure had not already been invented to describe the effect created by certain ladies, in bygone times, out of whalebone, elastic, foam rubber, rawhide thongs, and similar artificial devices, it would have to be coined today, to describe Dolly as Mother Nature created her.

There is a series of jokes in Nashville—they used to be part of her stage show—which involve Dolly discovering women's lib, deciding to burn her bra, and . . .

(a) it took her three days to finish the job.

(b) four volunteer fire departments from neighboring townships had to be called in to put it out.

(c) well, you get the idea—fill in your own punch line.

Or, consider the comment heard most frequently concerning the preparation of this book: You'll need two pages for every picture. . . .

Yet Dolly is a tiny, delicate creature, barely five feet tall, possessed of such open, unaffected charm and grace that one could almost forget her dimensions when talking to her. In fact, one interviewer after another seems to substantiate the idea that it's not hard to forget *everything* when talking to her:

"She could wear pajamas to a banquet," writes Jerry Bailey (quoted by Melvin Shestack in *The Country Music Encyclopedia*, 1974), "and many formally attired persons there would feel improperly dressed. In her presence, women tend to fidget with their hair and adjust their clothes; men stiffen uneasily and stare noticeably at the object of their admiration. She has a way of destroying one's composure, though it seems entirely unintentional."

Roy Blount, in *Esquire* (March, 1977) had the same experience: "Trying to think of something to say to Dolly in all her glory was, for me, like trying to think of something to say to a person who is coolly standing there on fire all over without being consumed."

And Chet Flippo (*Rolling Stone*, August 25, 1977) describes Mick Jagger, who should be, if anything is sacred in the world, too jaded to raise more than an eyebrow for any woman, upon being hugged by Dolly: "He looked for all the world like a twelve-year-old schoolboy blushing and gawking the first time a truly beautiful woman hugs him. Mick may be beyond purification, but he clearly experienced *something*."

Dolly Parton is a woman of paradoxes, and she seems to relish them. They give her yet another measure of control, and she is a person whose self-control, and self-directedness are phenomenal. So she is paradoxical. As she told Martha Hume, who complained to Dolly during an interview (*Us*, June 27, 1978) that she couldn't separate reality from fantasy in Dolly's stories about herself:

"Well, you never will...Nobody could ever know all of me. I'm even fascinatin' to myself, because I often do things that the day before I wouldn't have thought I would do."

Does she like having people wondering about her? Hume persisted.

"I guess I do, sorta... The more stories they tell, the more popular you become, the more curious people are about you. I don't want to tell it all, because if you know it all, then I wouldn't be fascinatin' to you. You might like me, but part of me is the fact that nobody knows."

So she is simple and complex, flamboyant and intensely private, sexy and pure. Even about her most famous anatomical characteristics, she told Chet Flippo: "There are going to be those who will say, 'I know that they're false, I knew her when', and there will be some who say, 'I know they're real.' I say: '*Let 'em guess.*'"

# DOLLY PARTON

Dolly wears her paradoxes as easily as she wears her wigs; and, as with her wigs, she makes the wildly improbable look completely natural on her. Because Dolly is her own woman, and has been, since she was five years old and dictating her first songs to her mother; since she was ten (or perhaps 13) and talking her way into an unscheduled appearance on the Grand Ole Opry; since she started singing duets with Porter Wagoner; since. . . .

And in fact, it's Dolly's propensity for being her own woman that is currently raising a lot of eyebrows in Nashville. And they've been raised ever since she became the first woman to cross over the boundaries of country and western music and make a solid bid for pop superstardom.

Does that mean that Dolly has sold out? Has she abandoned her roots? Has she left country to pursue success in the Sodom and Gomorrah of Hollywood and New York? Dolly claims she hasn't, but has she? Really? And why should anyone care, as long as she makes it work?

But people do care. Artistically, there are some who question whether her new pop style is as valid as the style that gave her her start. (Financially, it's hard to question—her latest album, *Here You Come Again*, has gone platinum, the first album by a woman country singer to even come near that mark.) And others care because . . . well, because they care. Country music is a way of life as much as it is a musical form, and its heroes and heroines are idolized by their fans, not just as performers, but as people. Like soap opera stars, they become practically part of the family of their fans. And as such, like any other member of the family, they are expected to behave themselves, and play out the role that has been assigned to them.

2

Country music is a way of life that is jealously guarded by its devotees. Traditionally, not just anyone could be recognized as a *country singer*. Singing songs with country themes or lyrics wasn't necessarily enough. Recording with guitars and banjos, or even a pedal steel guitar or a fiddle, wasn't enough. Not even recording in Nashville was enough—Perry Como had done that.

The first qualification was: you had to be 'country.' This is, you had to establish your credibility by having come from a country background, having paid your dues to the soil, poverty, and the South. You had to be a *good ole boy*. And, once having established that country credibility, it was virtually impossible to lose it.

Thus, by some people's standards anyway, Glen Campbell, a sharecropper's son from Delight, Arkansas, was accepted even though he had a network television show and sang songs about people needing people with a style that was as smooth as Robert Goulet's, while Kris Kristofferson, a Rhodes

17

scholar, was always regarded with a certain amount of suspicion even though his voice was as rough as a corncob and his songs were country masterpieces that the finest—and most traditional—singers in Nashville recognized, applauded, and recorded.

Actually, this distinction, while it had always existed, only became important in the sixties, because before that the only people who wanted to be country were the ones who couldn't be anything else. There was only a limited market for country music, and after the onslaught of Elvis and rock-and-roll in the fifties had changed the face of white music in America completely, even the market that had been there before shrank drastically.

But the popularity of country music began growing and spreading in the sixties and seventies. Johnny Cash had a nationwide television show; Bob Dylan went to Nashville to record *Nashville Skyline* album.

Before long it seemed as if everyone wanted to get into the act. The number of country music radio stations in America boomed. Where there had been a total of eighty throughout the country in 1960, by the early seventies there were that many in Tennessee alone, and nearly twice that many in Texas alone; across the country, there were over 1300 radio stations featuring country music, including stations in such outposts as New York City. Nashville had become the second largest recording center in the world, behind only New York.

There were a lot of people making records with Nashville musicians, or country themes, or country instrumentation, and a lot of them had never seen the backside of a mule. To the country music loyalists, the question of purity became important.

In 1974, Melvin Shestack's *The Country Music Encyclopedia* came out. Virtually every active

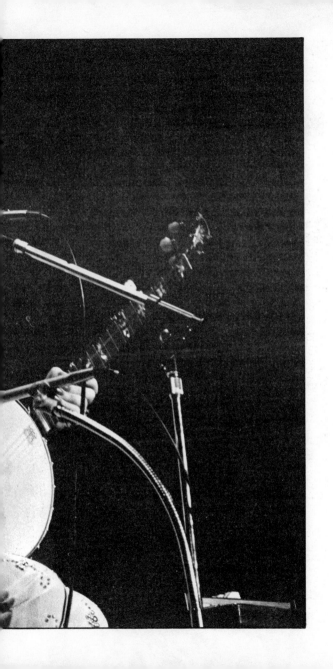

country music performer was included, and even a number not so active. Not included were a couple of highly successful pop stars, John Denver and Olivia Newton-John. They were not included simply because they were irrelevant. They had nothing to do with country music.

But later in that same year, the Country Music Association's award for Male Vocalist of the Year was given to none other than John Denver. And their female vocalist of the year was Olivia Newton-John.

These selections were widely denounced, not only by the old guard of country music fans, but by the traditional performers as well. A group of them went so far as to announce that they were splitting off from the Country Music Association and founding their own organization, the Association of Country Entertainers, which would make its own awards and promote the traditional values of country music. The leaders of this group were Hank Snow, George Morgan, Porter Wagoner . . . and Dolly Parton. Dolly, for her part, had some pointed and biting remarks to make about Hollywood types in general, and Olivia Newton-John in particular.

The Association of Country Entertainers turned out to be something of a tempest in a moonshine jug, although it did have the effect of bringing the Country Music Association back home. One of their own, Miss Dolly herself, was named Female Vocalist of the Year in both 1975 and 1976.

But by 1977, Dolly Parton was to find herself retracting a lot of her earlier comments—when she dropped her Nashville-based manager and hired the Hollywood management firm of Katz, Gallin and Cleary, managers of Mac Davis, Donny and Marie Osmond, Cher, Tony Orlando and Dawn, Kate Smith, and . . . Olivia Newton-John.

# DOLLY PARTON

That was the year that Dolly's career turned around with a suddenness that made people's heads spin. She began making regular appearances on The Tonight Show and "Hollywood Squares." She has just signed a three-movie deal with 20th Century Fox. Earl Wilson makes jokes about her bustline. She not only has Katz, Gallin and Cleary as managers, she has a new Hollywood booking agency, a new band made up of non-Nashville musicians, and a pop-music producer for her new album. She is less likely to be mentioned these days with Loretta Lynn and Tammy Wynette as one of the *big three* of country and western music, more likely to be linked with Linda Ronstadt and Emmylou Harris as one of the *big three* of pop.

And yet she still claims sensitivity to, and kinship with, the folks she appears to be leaving behind. And she still says repeatedly, as in this *Country Music* magazine interview (May, 1977) that she hasn't changed:

"I haven't turned my back on Nashville. I can't show them now that I haven't, but they'll see. They'll know. I will be able to do more for the name of country music by going ahead and doing what I feel I should do, by reaching a broader audience and as many people as I can and by having a universal appeal. I'll be able to do more for Nashville than I ever could have done had I stayed there."

3

Sorting out Dolly's history is an interesting exercise in trying to separate fact from legend. On the one hand, all sorts of improbable stories, like the one about her writing songs before she was five, turn out to be most likely true. On the other hand, perfectly simple details, like what her real hair looks like, or even what her husband looks like (never mind trying to find out any details about her marriage!) remain subjects for speculation, the simple facts shrouded in mystery.

What is known is that Dolly Rebecca Parton was born on January 19, 1946, in a two-room wooden shack in Sevier County, Tennessee, near the county seat of Sevierville, in the Smoky Mountains, and that she was delivered by Dr. Robert F. Thomas, who was later, for his troubles, to be rewarded with a song written about him by Dolly.

Dolly's sister, Willadeen Blalock, recalls it as an almost mystical event, and remembers Dolly as a baby so beautiful that the neighbors came from miles around just to see her. She does not mention anything about three wise men, but one suspects, nonetheless, that this story has been somewhat romanticized by the passage of time, or by Dolly's remarkable ability to turn everything around her into a fairy tale—not only her fairy princess appearance, and her own fantasies and recollections, but even other people's reminiscences about her childhood.

Dolly's early years were anything but a fairy tale. Even by the standards of rural hardship and poverty that one expects to find in the background of a country and western singer, the Partons' life style was particularly grim. (Loretta Lynn, the singer most often mentioned as Dolly's chief rival for the mythical crown of Queen of Country Music, is one of the few stars who can match Dolly, story for story, for downright, backwoods, empty-bellied, way-below-subsistence level, grinding poverty.)

Dolly was born, he was trying to make a living as Lee Parton, who had married as teenagers, and would have eight more before their family was complete, a total of six boys and six girls.

Robert Lee was a farmer, although at the time Dolly was born, he was trying to make a living as a construction worker. He soon went back to farming, though, and Dolly spent her early years on Webb Mountain, deep in the Smokies, where her father did his best to scratch out enough food for the family's survival from his little patch of stony mountain soil, and everyone in the Parton family, girls as well as boys, put in the same full day's work just to get enough to eat.

Avie Lee Parton married Robert at fifteen, and from then on, spent the rest of her youth taking care of one baby after another—she always had "one in her and one on her," as Dolly recalls it. It is the classic stereotype of rural poverty, and of women who get old and worn out before their times. But Avie Lee Parton is a strong, solidly built, square-jawed and handsome woman, in whose features one can see Dolly reflected clearly. In fact, looking at her mother, one realizes how strong and solid Dolly's fairy-princess features really are.

Dolly has often used her childhood and her roots as subject matter for her songs, especially in her album *My Tennessee Mountain Home*. Recorded in 1973, while Dolly was still with Porter, *My Tennessee Mountain Home* is a concept album—a collection of songs all tied together around a single theme.

It begins and ends with a *frame*—two songs that describe Dolly in Nashville, trying to break into the music business. In between those two, all the other songs on the album are a description of the old days, of her childhood in Tennessee, her fond memories of it, and her longing to return to its simple joys. It is an autobiographical album. Well, almost.

Rather, it is an extended piece of fiction—a story about a young woman from the Tennessee hills who has gone off to Nashville to become a star. But she keeps on dreaming of her idyllic childhood back in her Tennessee mountain home, and she keeps making plans to go back there, into the bosom of her family once again.

This young woman bears a striking resemblance to Dolly Parton. She comes from the same part of the country. She is one of twelve brothers and sisters—we are told that in two separate songs—and she was even brought into the world by the same doctor who delivered Dolly, the redoubtable Dr. Robert F. Thomas.

And everything on the album cover tends to reinforce the idea that the young woman being chronicled in the songs is, in fact, the real Dolly Parton. The cover photo is of a rural shack, with its

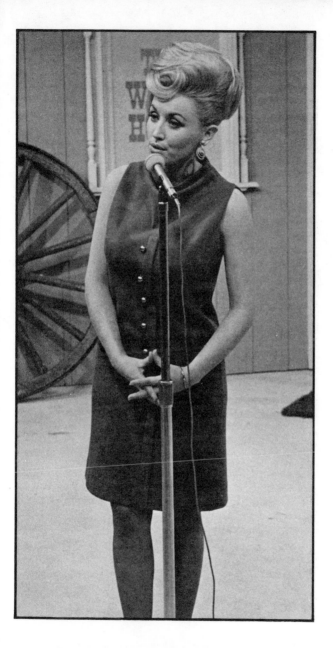

wringer washing machine on the front porch, auto parts and a few tin cans cluttering the dusty, stone-strewn front yard, and one scruffy bush of pink flowers that look vaguely like Rose of Sharon. It is *"My Tennessee Mountain Home—the house I lived in from the time I was five years old until I was ten years old. I remember these years most of all,"* as Dolly tells us on the album's liner notes.

There are also paintings of the log cabin Dolly was born in and of her Daddy's working boots (the subject of a song on the album), pictures of little Dolly at age four (log cabin days) and age seven (*Tennessee Mountain Home* days), pictures of Momma and Daddy, and pictures of Dolly, all grown up and bewigged, with Grandma and Grandpa Parton, Grandpa Owens, and even Dr. Robert F. Thomas.

Finally there are little reminiscences by Momma and Daddy, full of real and touching warmth and perfectly understandable platitudes, about how much they love Dolly and how proud of her they are.

Then there are the songs, most of which seem a little less easy to tie back into reality.

The first cut on the album is called "The Letter," and is simply Dolly reading, to the strains of "Be It Ever So Humble, There's No Place Like Home," the "first letter I wrote back home to Momma and Daddy, a few days after I got to Nashville."

Now, Dolly's singing voice is beautiful, but her speaking voice has a clear, childlike sincerity that would melt flint, and it's impossible to listen to her telling Momma and Daddy how much she misses them, but how determined to succeed she is, and how "I don't want you to worry about my gettin' in trouble . . . 'cause I'll be good, just like I promised you I would," without wanting to take her into your kitchen and give her a hot meal, and your phone number so she'll have someone to call on if she ever gets in trouble.

But much of the rest of the album loses that believability, although musically, it remains on a high level: In "I Remember," she describes "meadows . . . fields of golden wheat . . . songbirds . . . and sugar cane," plus gingerbread, toys, candy—it's just a little too perfect to be true.

Journalist Martha Hume describes the same problem with credibility as she describes an interview with Dolly in which "I listen to Parton describe [herself as] a little girl whose role could have been played by Shirley Temple.

"I grew up not far from where Parton did," Hume comments. "I know what mountain shacks look like, and they don't look like vine-covered cottages. I know what mountain children look like and they usually don't look like Shirley Temple. The land is pretty but the people aren't . . . of course, Parton knows this too . . . Still, I can't separate what is true about Parton from what is fantasy."

And the woman portrayed in the songs on the album keeps planning to go back home to the mountains, where her dear old Momma and Daddy are still waiting for her—unlike the real Dolly, who is quite clearly heading in the opposite direction—for Hollywood, the Johnny Carson show, prestigious concert stages like New York's Avery Fisher Hall. Whatever her fantasies of returning to the simple life in a little shack in the hills, away from "the factory smoke and city lights" that she rejects in the song "Back Home," the reality is that Dolly got out of the mountains as fast as she could, and she ain't going back.

Far closer to the truth, most likely, are these lines from "In the Good Old Days (When Times Were Bad)":

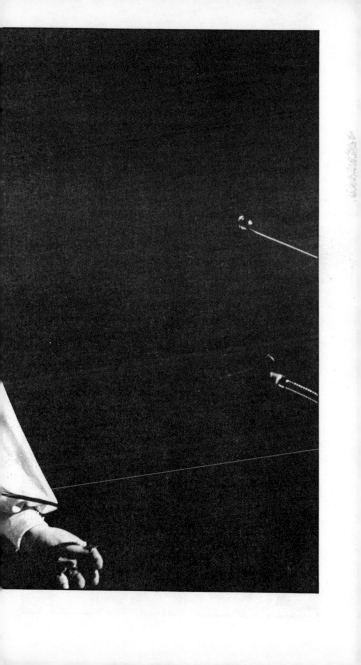

## DOLLY PARTON

No amount of money could buy from me
The memories that I have of then.
No amount of money could pay me
To go back and live through it again.

The unsparing, autobiographical honesty of this song makes it the most interesting on the album, with such lines as "I've seen Daddy's hands break open and bleed . . . I've seen Mama lyin' in sufferin' sickness, in need of a doctor we couldn't afford," contrasting sharply with the sugar-coated remembrances of many of the other songs.

One gets the feeling that Dolly is making a fairy tale, a make-believe world out of her own childhood, just as during her actual childhood, she had created a fantasy world in order to get some relief from the harsh realities of a childhood in which, as she told Joan Dew (in *Singers and Sweethearts: The Women of Country Music*, Doubleday, 1977): "We slept four in a bed and it didn't matter if you'd stopped wettin' 'cause someone else was gonna pee on you anyway." In a comic recitation that used to be part of her stage show, Dolly tells more about the bedwetting, which, she says, used to happen because in order to get twelve kids to go to bed and stay there, her parents used to frighten them with stories of monsters that lay in wait if they dared to get out of bed—"Ol' Scratch-Eye" who waited under the bed to leap out at a child who so much as dangled a foot over the edge, and "Ol' Bloody Bone" who lay in wait just outside the door.

Dolly's fantasy world was more than just scary stories and fairy tales, though—it was her songs, and her dreams, dreams that she was determined to make come true, of Nashville, a singing career, stardom. Her parents were not musical themselves, but they were supportive.

"One fine thing about Momma and Daddy," she told Joyce Maynard (*Good Housekeeping*, September, 1977), "is they always let their children hold onto their dreams. At first, Daddy didn't like the idea of me becoming a singer because he'd never heard tell of someone from our poor mountain background making it in the music business. But Mamma said from the beginning: "I bet you will be a star someday, honey."

Dolly was a self-starter, though, and even if she had to figure out music by herself, she was going to do it. Her intense, unwavering, single-minded determination to succeed seems to have been something she had right from infancy, because even as a toddler she was composing songs. She remembers making up her first songs before she was five, and before she could write them down herself, so that she had to get her mother to take them down from her dictation.

Of course, in any rural community where pre-packaged entertainment such as television, records, or movies is scarce, the music that people make themselves is the most common and widespread form of entertainment. Dolly's mother, although she was not a musician, did sing around the house —the old Appalachian ballads, descendants of the Elizabethan ballads that have been handed down from one generation to the next in the Smoky Mountains. These are the ballads of lost love and death, of betrayal and murder that come out of a culture that lives closely with loneliness and death, where primitive passions live side-by-side with stringent fundamentalist Christian morality. The songs have been popularized by folksingers like Joan Baez and the Kingston Trio—"Pretty Polly," "The Trees They Do Grow High," "Tom Dooley."

This traditional mountain folk music was much more a part of Dolly's musical upbringing than was the popular country and western music of the day, as represented by people like Hank Williams, Ernest Tubb, Lefty Frizzell and the other Grand Ole Opry stars. And this early influence still shows in her song writing. The old mountain themes of death and tragedy and loss come up again and again, in songs like "Me and Little Andy," "Jeannie's Afraid of the Dark," or "Down from Dover" (*The Best of Dolly Parton*, RCA LSP-4449 and *Mine*, Pickwick ACL-0307) in which a frightened pregnant girl waits for her lover to return from Dover and marry her, but in vain. Finally, when the baby is born, something seems wrong . . .

I hear no cryin'.
I guess in some strange way
She knew she'd never have
A father's arms to hold her,
And dyin' was her way of tellin' me
He won't be coming
Down from Dover....

In another, chilling, more contemporary adaptation of the classic Gothic story structure, she writes and sings of the kind of powerlessness of a woman in the grip of the male-dominated social structure common to so much of her audience. The song is called "Daddy, Come And Get Me" (*The Best of Dolly Parton*). The opening words—"In this mental institution"—delivered in Dolly's best heart-tugging, brave-little-soldier style, immediately plunge the listener into the song's world of unrelieved, helpless despair. The woman in the song has been suddenly and cruelly told by her husband that he is leaving her for another woman, and that he wants a divorce. She refuses, and he takes advantage of her grief and pain-induced hysteria to have her committed: "I cried and cried for days / And he said that I was crazy, but he just put me in here to get me out of his way."

"I need help," she pleads, "but not this kind." But she can't help herself. And she is left clinging to only one faint, desperate hope, that of rescue by another man—her father—who up until this point has not even seemed to be interested enough in her to find out where she is.

"Daddy, come and get me," she begs.

> ... You said that I could come to you
> if I ever was in need,
> But Daddy, I can't come to you,
> so you'll have to come to me.

# DOLLY PARTON

In addition to the mountain songs that her mother sang, Dolly had another chief musical influence: that cornerstone of rural life, and rural music, the church.

Dolly's was the House of Prayer, and the minister was her grandfather, also known as Brother Jake Owens. Dolly was later to celebrate him in a song she recorded with Porter Wagoner, "Daddy Was an Old-Time Preacher Man," in which the old-time preacher is described as preaching "Hell so hot that you could feel the heat."

Brother Jake didn't fool around. "I remember the hell-fire and brimstone he used to preach," Dolly told Chet Flippo, and how I used to be *real* scared of that and I think that inspired me or *depressed* me into writin' all those sad, mournful songs. You kind of grew up in a horrid atmosphere about this fear of religion. We thought God was a *monster* in the sky."

But even with God as a kind of cosmic Scratch-Eye, the House of Prayer became one of Dolly's chief avenues for expressing herself in song. She sang at church, and she kept on singing at home, too.

When she was seven, she made herself her first instrument, a home-made guitar. It was put together out of the materials she had on hand—the body of an old mandolin and two bass guitar strings. It was an unlikely instrument, but she coaxed notes and simple chords out of it. And she went on writing songs.

The next year, when she was eight, she got her first real guitar, from Brother Jake's son, her uncle Bill Owens, who was to play a large role in encouraging and helping her career. But the encouragement she received at home from her family was not always reinforced by everyone she knew.

At the same time, her life in Sevierville was leaving childhood scars on her that would be many years in healing.

One of Dolly Parton's best known songs, and perhaps the finest of all of her songs, is the haunting and touching "Coat of Many Colors," about the hurt, loneliness and confusion of a little child tormented by the cruelty and snobbishness of her schoolmates.

"Coat of Many Colors" (*Coat of Many Colors*, RCA LSP-4603 and *Best of Dolly Parton*, RCA APLI-1117) tells the story of Dolly, at age eight, going to school to have her picture taken for a class photograph. Her family was too poor to afford a new coat for her to wear, or even to afford the material to make a new coat. But her mother did have a box of scraps of material that had been given to her by a neighbor, scraps that were too small to make anything with. But Mrs. Parton figured that if she sewed all the scraps together, she'd have enough to make a coat.

As she worked at the sewing, so Dolly tells the story, her mother told her the tale of Joseph in the Bible, and how his father had loved him so much

49

that he made him a coat of many colors. (Incidentally, it's a good thing that Dolly's mother had that old family Bible—if she'd had the Revised Standard Version, she would have discovered that Joseph's coat, in the more accurate but less poetic translation of the newer version, was merely a coat with long sleeves.)

All that love, the Biblical love and the love her mother "sewed in every stitch" of the coat, soon had Dolly feeling as if she must be just about the most special person in the Smoky Mountains, to have such a wonderful garment made just for her. She couldn't wait to wear it to school, and when it was finally ready she hurried off to the schoolhouse, wearing it, only to find to her shame and bewilderment that her classmates just laughed at her and made fun of her.

Dolly couldn't understand the reception

... for I felt I was rich,
And I told them of the love my Mama sewed
   in every stitch,
And I told them of the story Mama told me
   when she sewed,
And how my coat of many colors was worth
   more than all their clothes.

In the song, the children continue not to understand how special the coat is, and they go on laughing at her and making fun of her. In real life, as Dolly told Chet Flippo, it was even worse than that—"a very sad and cutting memory that I long kept deep within myself ... How the kids tried to take my little coat off and I was just sprouting ... boobs, you know, and I didn't have a blouse on under it because I had done *well* just to have a jacket to wear. So when the kids kept sayin' I didn't have a shirt on under it, I said I *did* because

# DOLLY PARTON

I was embarrassed. So they broke the buttons off
my coat. They locked me in the coat closet that day
and held the door closed and it was black dark in
there and I just went into a screaming fit. I remem-
bered all that and I was ashamed to even mention
it and for *years* I held it in my mind."

It is a painful and bitter memory, no doubt about
it. And all those years of holding it in, the time
and the pain that it took before she could finally
break through and face the incident squarely
enough to write about, are reflected in this finely
crafted song.

"Back through the years I go wand'rin' once
again" is the haunting, evocative opening. That is
an unusual opening for a Parton story song—
almost all the others get right into the action from
the first word. But here, she's hesitant. The story
doesn't start until the third line. And by the time it
does, we already know a few things about what is
coming up. We know that this is memory that has
been relived over and over—and from the way
that she delays in starting the story, we get a sense
of how hard it is, still, for her to bring the memory
up at all.

Listening to Dolly sing "Coat of Many Colors" in
concert, one can hardly fail to be moved by how
deeply felt the memory is. No matter how often she
sings it, she seems to be discovering the pain all
over again each time.

And in fact, that same childhood experience may
have spawned yet another of her best songs, in-
directly. Ever since the day that she was locked
in that dark closet at school, Dolly has been afraid
of the dark, and even today, she always sleeps
with a light on. And her eerily disturbing duet with
Porter Wagoner, "Jeannie's Afraid Of The Dark,"
deals with this same fear.

And yet—the "and yet" that seems to go with

almost every Dolly Parton story—there's another half to the Bible story of Joseph and his coat of many colors (even if it was only a coat with long sleeves). And it has its own relevance to Dolly's story. Joseph's coat was no better received than Dolly's. Worse, in fact.

And in Joseph's case, it was his own brothers who did him in. When they saw him in the coat, the first thing they did was to beat him up. Then they stole the coat, colors, sleeves and all. Then they sold him into slavery.

Of course, Joseph's coat was a symbol of wealth, and Dolly's a symbol of poverty. But even more important than the wealth, Joseph's was a symbol of special favor, and that's what made his brothers resent him so. Joseph had gotten himself in trouble with his brothers already, by telling them about a dream he'd had where they were all binding sheaves of wheat, and everyone else's sheaf bowed down before his sheaf. The coat, symbolizing that his father loved him best of all his sons, was the last straw.

And even in Dolly's sad, touching song, there's some indication that Dolly felt somewhat the same way about herself—her coat of many colors, she tells her classmates, is "worth more than all their clothes," and she can't understand why they won't recognize that.

Her sister Willadeen remembers how Dolly sensed her specialness at an early age, and the price she paid for it. "She had her dreams of stardom from a very early age," Willadeen told Joan Dew, "and she wasn't shy about telling them. Where we lived in the hills, nobody had dreams like that, so naturally the kids laughed."

And it was more than just her dreams of stardom that got her into trouble with her peers. "I was a homely little thing," she has said of herself as a child—Willadeen's memory of the baby so beautiful that the neighbors flocked around in wonder notwithstanding. But if she was, she certainly did not stay homely for long—nor did her famous figure suddenly develop out of nowhere after she had graduated from high school and left Sevierville for Nashville.

And, as could be expected in any high school in America, that kind of spectacular figure can create it's own built-in problems.

"I was the most popular girl in school in the *wrong way*," she told Chet Flippo. "*Everybody* talked about Dolly but I didn't have as many friends as I should have ... I had a lotta stories told on me, a lotta lies, just because I looked the way I did. I was always big in the boobs, small in the waist, and big in the butt. I just grew up that way and had that *foxy* personality, too ... I always wore tight clothes. When I walked down the hall, everybody was a-lookin' to see how tight my skirt was that day or how tight my sweater was. I never did like to go around half naked but a lotta people said I might as well be naked, as tight as my clothes were. But even as a little bitty kid, if my mama made me wear somethin' that was loose on me, I used to just cry. I wanted my clothes to fit me. Even though they was just rags, I wanted them to fit close to me."

It must have been difficult for Dolly in her teenage years, growing up foxy in a Fundamentalist home where the Blood of the Lamb was the only animal likely to be accepted as a symbolic behavior model.

Dolly did her best, though. When her father refused to let her wear lipstick, she put Mercurochrome on her lips. If you've never tried putting Mercurochrome on your lips, a good piece of advice is—don't. Not unless you're convinced that you want red lips so badly that you're willing to make the sacrifice of a considerable amount of pain to reach that goal.

Dolly was more than willing to pay the price, and she got what she wanted. The Mercurochrome wouldn't come off. And there was nothing her father could do about it. But one is reminded of the story of the ancient Spartan boy who brought his pet fox with him to his first day in the army, hid the animal under his coat, and then let it eat his stomach out rather than blow his image by falling out of attention in line and appearing less than the perfect soldier.

Dolly is fond of referring to herself as a "brave little soldier," and the image is an apt one, except that the marching orders she has obeyed have always been her own. Still, she expects and demands the same kind of self-discipline and consistency from others. "When I was a little girl," she told Joyce Maynard, "going to the movies was considered sinful in our neck of the woods. But when a movie called *Thunder Road*—a true Tennessee story that was filmed right near us and starred Robert Mitchum—came to town, Daddy said that we could go. I was tickled to death, of course, but it also made me feel so sad. I didn't enjoy the movie. Up until that night, Mama and Daddy were my heroes, and it seemed like they'd broken their own rules."

Dolly obeyed the rules—stretching them as far as she could. And she is unstinting in her praise for her parents and their rules and values. But at the same time, she has admitted: "I never felt I belonged...I was just *different*, and so I never really found my place till I moved to Nashville and got in the music business."

# DOLLY PARTON

## 6

Dolly's Uncle Bill Owens, who had bought her her first guitar, believed in her career. Listening to her sing around the house, and in church, he thought he heard something special in her voice, and something worth promoting. When she was barely more than a toddler (ten years old according to his memory, seven according to hers), he took her down to Knoxville, Tennessee, twenty miles from Sevierville, to audition for Cass Walker, a popular local radio personality.

At Dolly's audition, Owens remembers, "announcers and other people from all over the building came in, announcers from upstairs and everywhere, just to hear this new talent. She was an instant hit, and Cass signed her on the spot."

She became a regular guest on Walker's show, and she and her uncle were inspired to even greater heights of ambition. He arranged for her to cut a record for a small Southern label called Gold Band, headquartered in Lake Charles, Louisiana. The song was called "Puppy Love," and it was coauthored by Dolly and her uncle, who was to coauthor several of the songs on her first real album, after she came to Nashville. The distribution was about what you would expect from a label headquartered in Lake Charles, Louisiana, and the record was universally ignored. But Bill Owens and Dolly had another string to their bow. They decided to try to get Dolly into the Grand Ole Opry.

"When I was ten," Dolly told Joyce Maynard (although, as we've seen, these early dates are a little shaky—other memories make her thirteen), "my uncle borrowed a car and drove me to Nashville. I wore a blue silk dress he'd bought me."

They drove to Ryman Auditorium, at that time the home of the Grand Ole Opry, arriving just in time for the Friday night broadcast. Somehow, Dolly managed to march past the security guards, guitar in hand, and get backstage.

Backstage at the Opry! That would have been the thrill of a lifetime, in itself, for most Southern kids.

But not for Dolly. Nothing would satisfy her but the impossible—going on and performing on the Opry show.

She made sure that everyone knew about it, and everyone told her the same thing—no way! It was impossible, out of the question! Get lost, kid! But she persisted—it's a wonder that she wasn't just thrown out of the theater. And finally Opry regular Jimmy "C." Newman, whose hit, "A Fallen Star" was riding the charts at the time, let her go on and sing during his segment.

"I sang 'If You Want to Be My Baby,'" she recalls. "And I kept thinking about Mama and Daddy and all my brothers and sisters back home, listening to me on the radio. When I finished my song, the audience just clapped and clapped like I always knew they would."

It was to be a while, though, before she would hear that sort of applause again. Dolly was not destined to be an overnight success at ten. It was back to Sevierville, back to school and to poverty. (Although around the time that she was ten, her father had begun to do a little better. They were able to buy a larger farm, around forty to fifty acres, in an area called Caton's Chapel, and Dolly lived there until she graduated from high school.)

She still had her sights fixed unblinkingly on Nashville and stardom. But it would have to wait until she had finished high school. Her parents were absolutely strict on that score, and she went along with them.

On the day of her graduation, as Willadeen describes it, at the graduation ceremony "the students were asked to get up and tell their plans for the future, and of course Dolly said she was going off to Nashville to become a singer. You could hear the snickers all through the audience."

But it was no joke to Dolly. The next morning, with a cardboard suitcase and a fistful of songs, she was on the bus to Nashville.

Bill Owens had preceded her there. About two weeks before Dolly graduated, he had pulled up stakes, moved his wife and baby to Nashville, and found an apartment with room enough for Dolly to move in with them when she arrived. So the move to Nashville was something of a family project. Dolly did, in fact, move in with the Owenses, and lived with them for five months, while she pounded doors on Music Row and looked for a break.

Five months was all it took for Dolly to get that first foot in the door. She got a song writing contract with Monument Records and Combine Music, which gave her a small weekly salary. It was enough to allow her the independence of her own apartment, so she moved out of her uncle's place.

Fred Foster, president of Monument Records, recognized Dolly's talent right away, but was not quite sure what to do with it.

Dolly's voice has a uniquely clear, shimmering purity of tone—part childlike, part otherworldly, and Foster was not convinced that it was adaptable to the rough-and-ready, everyday life themes of the country music of the mid-sixties. Hits by women singers that year had been songs like Tammy Wynette's "Apartment Number Nine" and Loretta Lynn's "Don't Come Home A-Drinkin' (With Lovin' on Your Mind)."

Foster experimented on Dolly with other musical styles, recording her with a rock accompaniment which she could in no way relate to.

"Monument Records was doing what it thought best at the time," she told Jerry Bailey. "They didn't think I could possibly sell any country because they thought I sounded like a little girl. They didn't think I could sell any hard message song or sad story, because no one would believe it. But I always wanted to do it, so I told them after a while that I was going to do what I felt I could do in my heart or I was going to have to leave."

Today, of course, in her newest albums, Dolly has gone very much into the rock idiom, sparking the controversy over whether or not she is still "country"; but Dolly today is a very different person from the girl from Sevierville who came into Nashville on a bus, clutching a cardboard suitcase, out of a backwoods home that allowed no movies, no television, no records, no juke joints, and radio only for the Saturday night broadcast of the Grand Ole Opry.

## DOLLY PARTON

There were a couple of very lean years in Nashville for Dolly, even with her Monument contract. She recalls one stretch of three weeks during which she lived on nothing but mustard and hamburger relish. Her husband-to-be, Carl Dean, whom she had met her first day in Nashville, was away in the Army, and "the only time I ever got a really good meal was when I was on a date, and I didn't date anybody in the music business that much, because I didn't want to get a reputation. Not that I would have done anything to get one, but you don't have to, really."

Fred Foster finally decided to take a chance on Dolly with a country song, and gave her a tune called "Dumb Blonde," written by an established Nashville songwriter named Curly Putnam, who also wrote "Green, Green Grass of Home," the great hit for future partner, Porter Wagoner. It was a hit, and Dolly was on her way.

The song also gave Dolly a totally inappropriate tag that has stuck with her, more or less, over the years. The cover line on the June 27, 1978 issue of *Us* magazine for their Dolly Parton story is the refrain line from the song: "This dumb blonde ain't nobody's fool."

Monument has recently reissued the first album Dolly made for them, in the wake of her current crest of popularity (*In the Beginning*, Monument MG 7623), and it makes for very instructive, if not entirely rewarding, listening.

For a start, it's a little misleading, in that it shows a very sophisticated, 1978-vintage Dolly on the cover, while the singer represented inside is anything but.

In fact, the first time I played the record, a visiting friend, who didn't know what jacket I had pulled it out of, thought for sure that it was Brenda

# DOLLY PARTON

Lee, and was only persuaded with difficulty that it was Dolly Parton.

It's clear, in this early record, that the dilemma of what to do with Dolly's strange voice had not yet been resolved in favor of not tampering with it. Monument was still trying to mold her into a proven commercially successful image, but all they really succeeded in doing was producing a good imitation of an ordinary, undistinguished country sound.

In the Beginning is noteworthy also in that it is the only Dolly Parton album on which the best song ("Dumb Blonde") is also the only one that she did not write.

All the other songs on the album are by Dolly, in most cases in collaboration with her uncle, Bill Owens. And, as with her singing voice, they are all aimed at fitting into an accepted, standard country music mold, but one which was not Dolly. All of them have typical country-song *hooks*, or catchy refrain lines, delivered with the sort of conventional arrangement that has a chorus come in to punch up the hook: "Every time you touch me you add *fuel to the flame*," or "You're known by *the company you keep*," or "*Put off until tomorrow*, you've hurt me enough today."

Actually, In the Beginning is not really a bad album—in some ways, some might argue, it's better than a recent album like New Harvest ... First Gathering in that it's less pretentious and more consistent. And it has its charming moments, like the artless understatement (in "Somethin' Fishy," which was Dolly's first hit with a song that she wrote herself): "I guess some widemouthed bass left that lipstick on your shirt / I don't think that you're a fisherman, I think that you're a flirt."

And in "The Company You Keep," in which an

older sister lectures her younger sister on the perils of acquiring a bad reputation, the flair for characterization within the framework of a song, later developed so brilliantly in songs like "My Blue Ridge Mountain Boy" or "Down From Dover," can be seen. But basically, *In the Beginning* is just that—a beginning, a warmup for a singer/songwriter who was still finding her voice.

To get ahead of the story a little, in 1967, when Dolly was offered the job of girl singer in Porter Wagoner's show, which involved going out on the road with Porter for the traditional grueling series of one-nighters (on stage, that is), a number of people who had been her self-appointed advisors on her career told her, "Aren't you glad you're not married, or you couldn't go." And she replied, "Well, I am married, and I am going!"

Dolly was married then, and had been married for a year, but nobody knew about it. That's a little unusual, but not strikingly so; after all, lots of people, especially people in show business, do get secretly married and keep their marriages a secret for one reason or another, usually having to do with their wanting to keep up the illusion of being single in order to fuel the fantasies of their fans of the opposite sex.

In Dolly's case, however, the people she knew and the people she worked with not only didn't know that she was married, but had they been told she was married, they also would not have known, or even been able to guess, to whom.

That is a little more unusual. Even if you're keeping your marriage a secret, your friends and associates at least generally tend to know who you're going around with.

But still, it's not beyond the realm of credibility. What *is* remarkable about Dolly's marriage is that today, twelve years later, most of the people that Dolly is closest to in her professional life *still* don't know who Dolly is married to.

Well, they know his name. Carl Dean. And that he is a contractor, a partner in his father's asphalt paving business.

Beyond that, nothing. Joan Dew, in 1977, reported that after three years of interviewing almost everyone in the music business in Nashville, she could find only four people who had ever seen Carl Dean, and no one who had much to say about him: teenage country star Tanya Tucker described him as "real nice," singer Jeannie Pruett as "handsome," and Fred Foster as "quiet and good-looking."

Loretta Lynn says of Carl: "I've never set eyes on him. And she never talks about her marriage. I've told her all about *mine*."

And in 1977, Chet Flippo was able to get a rise out of Dolly by asking her if Carl really existed. He does, of course. But most people still have to take it on faith.

Dolly met Carl Dean on the day she arrived in Nashville from Sevierville. She had stopped at a Nashville establishment called the Wishy-Washy Laundromat to wash some clothes that she had scooped up dirty in her last-minute haste to leave home, and she was standing outside the laundromat, drinking a Coke and looking at the street scene of the big city, when a handsome young man in a white Chevy drove past.

Dolly has told this story many, many more times than there are people in Nashville who have seen Carl Dean. How the handsome young man waved at her, and she waved back—not flirting, just being friendly, like country folks. And how he drove around the block and came back, parked the car, and began talking to her.

"I wouldn't get in the car with him or anything—we're not *that* friendly in the country." But she gave him her uncle's address, and Carl came around and began courting. They dated for a few months, and then Carl had to go into the Army.

By the time he returned, Dolly's career was starting to move. She had signed with Monument Records, and things were a good deal different than they had been when Carl had left town for the Army.

He still wanted to marry her. And she had known long before he had left for the service that Carl was the man she wanted to marry. But they had a lot to talk over, before they made the decision.

Carl was not the slightest bit interested in the music business, and he knew nothing about it. Dolly had to explain to him what it would be like to be married to a singer, one who was uncompromisingly dedicated to her music and her career. The touring, the long separations. The publicity, the gossip, the rumors. And the long, grueling hours of work, the intense concentration that would absorb so much of her waking hours. And he had to understand that this was not a passing fancy for Dolly, something that she would pursue for a few years, and then abandon in favor of a "normal" life in the kitchen and the country club.

And it would probably mean no children—not with the demands of touring and being away from home that are put on a singer. Loretta Lynn has children, but she had her family started before she began her singing career. And her younger children have grown up hardly knowing their mother, a source of pain and trial for all concerned. Dolly did not want to let the same thing happen to her.

"Any other man would probably have thought I was crazy," she told Joan Dew, "a kid from the hills talking about all these big plans like they had already happened—but Carl accepted it."

The story is that Carl Dean has never seen his wife perform. That may be a slight exaggeration— "He *has* seen me perform," she told Chet Flippo. "And he liked it. So there." But, on the other hand, she told Joan Dew, with a giggle, "He doesn't even like the way I sing." So *there*.

So there is Carl Dean, somewhere there, somewhere in his own world of asphalt paving, and strictly out of his wife's professional world, by his own choice. He and Dolly never entertain, have never so much as invited anyone in the music business over for a drink.

Carl went to one show business function with her, shortly after they were married. It was an awards banquet given by BMI, the songwriters' and composers' organization, during which Dolly was to get an award for one of her songs, the first such honor she had ever received. She was excited but nervous, and she sked Carl to go with her.

He went—for the first, last and only time. When they got home, he told her, "Now I know that this is what you want for your life and I'm proud of you because it makes you happy. But it don't make me happy and I don't want to be a part of it ... if anything ever comes up in your business that I

want to go to I'll tell you, but otherwise don't ask me."

And in the twelve years of their marriage, Dolly reports, "He hasn't asked to go to anything ... and I haven't asked him, so it's worked out fine."

The unusual nature of their marriage has produced its share of inevitable rumors. It has been gossiped around that theirs was strictly a marriage of convenience—that Dolly wanted to have the pressure of being a single woman on the road taken off her. It has even been said that Dolly wanted to be married in order to keep Porter from getting any ideas about her. But this would seem to be giving too much credit for advanced planning to even someone as formidably prepared for everything as Dolly, since she and Carl had been married for over a year before she ever met Porter.

It has been said that she offered Carl a deal—half her earnings in exchange for the social security of a marriage in name only.

And of course, during her years as a member of the Porter Wagoner Show, there were widespread rumors to the effect that she and Porter were lovers.

These she denies flatly. She and Porter were certainly close during the years they were together, and Dolly admits that the closeness was more than just professional. There was, she says, a deep bond of love and respect between them, but she insists that "I could fall asleep on the same bed with Porter and we'd never touch as male and female are supposed to."

Dolly does not see anything strange about her relationship with Carl. For her, she says, it works perfectly. Her professional life is one thing, and her life with Carl is her refuge from it. She can let her hair down with Carl—literally as well as figuratively. Well, more or less. She told Joyce

Maynard, "I never wear a wig when we're alone. I tie my own hair, which is kind of brownish, on top of my head. Carl likes me more natural."

This apparently innocuous detail, curiously enough, makes Carl privy to one of the few sights in Nashville rarer than Carl himself—his wife's hair. Loretta Lynn put it this way, to Roy Blount: "All of the girls streak the whole dressing room. But with Dolly, there's always a little curtain she pulls. I have never seen her without her wig. Don't know anyone who has. I don't even know what color her hair is."

Shortly after Carl and Dolly married, they sent for Dolly's four youngest brothers and sisters, still living at home in the mountains, and took them into their home in Nashville. They raised them and took care of them—which mostly means that Carl raised them and took care of them—until the youngest was grown and married, just a couple of years ago. One of Dolly's younger sisters, Stella, is now trying to carve out a career of her own. She has not had the spectacular success of Loretta Lynn's younger sister, Crystal Gayle, now challenging Loretta for the honor of star of the family, but she has had a couple of respectably selling records.

As for Dolly's life on the road, and its effect on her marriage—well, she's still married. Whatever may or may not have happened between her and Porter, whatever kinds of temptation Dolly finds in her path when she's out on the road, and how she responds to them, are at best subjects for speculation and gossip, nothing firmer. Anyone who guards her private life and personal privacy as tightly as Dolly does, is not likely to volunteer any true confessions on the subject of extramarital affairs.

She does, however, appear to be acknowledg-

ing that the gossip exists, and she seems to be making an answer to it, in a beautiful, sensually aware song called "He Would Know" (*The Bargain Store*, RCA APL 1-0950).

*The Bargain Store* is one of the last Porter-Dolly collaborative efforts—the singing is all solo Dolly, but the production and the band are Porter's, and one of his songs is included on the record. "He Would Know," however, doesn't sound like a song about Dolly and Porter, but more like an infatuation of the road, a secret crush and sexual longing that's still being resolved in the singer's mind.

Of course, it is true that Dolly has always mixed autobiography with slightly restructured autobiography in her songs. But what she says in "He Would Know" is that the temptation, strong as it is, desirable though the object of her fantasies is, still cannot quite be worth giving in to.

She acknowledges the fantasies openly—"In my mind I've made love to you a thousand times" is the opening line of the song. "You're someone very special . . . making love to you would be so easy . . ." but she won't do it, because:

> He would know
> Yes, he could tell
> For he has loved me long enough to know me
>   very well
> And if I lie
> He'd see it in my eyes
> I know my guilt would show, and he would
>   know.

The terms of the conflict, and the resolution, are set up in the strongest possible terms. The sensuality of the woman's feelings, the naked strength of the attraction, are stated clearly and simply in the words, and the little-girl openness of Dolly's delivery make the message even clearer.

But the resolution is just as satisfying. It seems a good enough reason for not giving way to the temptation, but no buffer at all against feeling it.

It's not hard to believe anything Dolly sings, and one can very easily come away from listening to "He Would Know" convinced that it is the story of every infatuation that ever crossed Dolly's mind. But then what do we make of this?

"That's not sayin' I ain't made mistakes and won't make mistakes," she said cryptically in a conversation with Chet Flippo about the lyrics and situation behind "He Would Know." "But if I can just write it and say this is a song about our situation, I hope you can better understand how I feel about it and why it can't be."

"I've written a lot of songs about heartbreak and love gone bad," she has said in talking about her relationship with her husband, "But Carl and I have never had an argument. I know we'll always be together. I wouldn't want to learn another man the way I've learned Carl. There's not another man in the world that can give me what I need."

On the other hand, she told Pete Axthelm of *Newsweek*: "I need my husband for love, and other men for my work. But I don't depend on any man for my strength."

Porter Wagoner is one of the biggest, longest-lasting, and most dependable of country stars. He has been making hit records for twenty-five years, solid, dependable, mainstream country hits like "Green, Green Grass of Home," "A Satisfied Mind," and "The Cold Hard Facts of Life."

Porter is exactly the kind of star that people mean when they talk about the old-fashioned, traditional country and western music personality, the "hillbilly" performer, the pre-Mac Davis, Glen Campbell, John Denver. Born in West Plains, Missouri, in 1927. A depression childhood. Quit school in the seventh grade to support his family, drove a truck before truck drivers began to be mythologized as the new knights of the road—for that matter, before he was old enough to have any business driving a truck.

Got his start in show business when he was working in a butcher shop back in West Plains, when the owner heard him singing "Jimmy Brown, the Newsboy" as he worked in the back room. The butcher decided that Porter was just the ticket, went around to the local West Plains radio station, bought himself a fifteen-minute, early morning slot, and Porter was in business—*"Just tell 'em what our specials for the day are and sing a few songs."*

"People must have felt sorry for me," Porter recalls, because it was unbelievable the amount of mail I got." And then, the inevitable in these stories, too corny to be true, but it couldn't possibly be anything *but* true—"One morning I went down to the store to open up to do the radio show and there was this big black Lincoln setting in front of the store."

*"Come here, boy, I'm gonna make you a star..."*

By 1961, Porter had his own syndicated television show, shown throughout the South and Midwest, sponsored by a good old Southern company, the Chattanooga Medicine Company, makers of patent medicines with names like "Black Draught" and "The Wine of Cardui." And it became the most popular of all syndicated country music shows with the exception of *Hee Haw*; it reached some forty-five million viewers.

As Porter said when he was asked by popular Nashville radio personality and interviewer Ralph Emery, on *Opry Star Spotlight*, for the secret of his success: "I guess it 'uz 'cuz I was a *sin*-cere person."

And in 1967, Porter was looking for a new female vocalist for his act—his television show and his traveling stage show.

For the previous seven years, he had been using a popular country singer named Norma Jean, who had built up a following of her own and was well-liked by Porter's audiences. But Norma Jean had decided to get married and settle down. She was going to have to cut down on her touring, so she told Porter she was leaving.

# DOLLY PARTON

Porter tried out a few other girl singers—including Tammy Wynette—but the chemistry just wasn't there.

Dolly had recorded several songs for Monument by this time, and had minor hits with songs like "Dumb Blonde" and "Somethin' Fishy." Porter decided to give her a try. He called her and asked her to come by and see him.

Porter has described that first meeting so often that it has become permanently engraved in the stone tablets of *great country legends*:

"Dolly came to my office, but she really didn't know what we were going to talk about. She brought her guitar. And she sang a song for me, a song about everything being beautiful. She had written it. And this song told me so much about her. I knew if a person could sit down and write a song like that, they'd have to have a real soul inside 'em."

Dolly had brought her guitar to Porter's office on the assumption that he was auditioning her songs. Dolly still thought of herself primarily as a writer in those days. She and her uncle had formed their own publishing company, Owepar Music, and Dolly had been devoting much of her time and energy to trying to sell her songs around town. In fact, she had sent several of them to Wagoner's organization, and she had heard a rumor that Norma Jean was interested in one of them, and might want to record it.

When Dolly heard that Porter was thinking, not of buying one of her songs for Norma Jean, but of hiring her as Norma Jean's replacement, it was the opportunity of a lifetime—and it presented her with the prospect of an overwhelming change in her life. It sounds glib and easy when she tells the story now—"*They said, 'Aren't you glad you're not married, or you couldn't go, and I said, 'Well,*

*I am married, and I am going' "*—but it can't have been as easy as it sounds.

It was marriage, after all, that had taken Norma Jean off the show. She didn't think that the demands of marriage and her commitment to Porter were compatible, and neither, one presumes, did her husband. And Dolly, too, was a Southern girl, coming from a long and firmly entrenched, traditionally conservative culture, where women's liberation has never exactly become a household word.

More than that, she was married to a man who was not even in the music business, from which vantage point he might have had a basis for being able to relate to the experience. He was a small-town Southern contractor, set in his ways, set in his interests, set in his values.

It was one thing that they had talked over all of these possibilties before they got married, and that Carl had agreed that Dolly should pursue her career. That was an agreement to something abstract, a vague possibility. The odds against success in any form of show business are astronomical. And back in the mid-sixties, it was still especially difficult for women to make it big in country music. The conventional wisdom was that since women were the big buyers of country records, they would only be interested in male singers. The men would fuel their fantasies, the women would only inflame their jealousies. Beyond Kitty Wells and Patsy Cline, it would be difficult to name any other country women who had become big stars. The big three of female country music—Loretta Lynn, Tammy Wynette, and Dolly—were about to change that, but no one knew it yet. Carl Dean could not possibly have known what he was getting into.

This is just the beginning of what being a regular on the Porter Wagoner show meant:

# DOLLY PARTON

Being out on the road for fifteen to twenty days every month.

Over a hundred one-night stands, in small towns and cities all over the country, in a year.

Grueling days and nights of bus travel.

Long hours in the television and recording studios during the time that she did get off the road, and back to Nashville.

Plus publicity appearances, plus award banquets, plus industry functions, plus interviews and press conferences and conferences with producers, songwriters, etc. Even without the strains of keeping up a marriage to consider, the strains on an ordinary person's constitution are immense.

Thanks to the Robert Altman movie *Nashville*, and the character played by Ronee Blakely who was based—fairly accurately—on Loretta Lynn, the American public knows all about Loretta's periodic nervous collapses and rest cures in sanitariums. But it's less generally known that such problems are not restricted to frail and emotionally delicate ladies like Loretta Lynn. Even an old toughie like Porter Wagoner can fall victim to nervous collapse from total exhaustion, and the strains of the road and the constant pressure of performance. And Porter has had his share of breakdowns, probably as many as Loretta. The strain of the road almost killed Johnny Cash. It did kill Hank Williams.

And the strain on a marriage can be disastrous in the life of any performer, male or female. But for a woman, especially a country woman, dealing with the traditional demands on a woman's place in a marriage, it can be especially rough. Tammy Wynette has had four husbands. Loretta Lynn is still with the man she married when she was thirteen, but she admits openly that it's a disaster—she has become a kind of landlocked Flying Dutch-

man, spending almost all her time in her bus, on the road, so she won't have to go home.

But as far as Dolly was concerned, that had all been decided before she got married, and she was ready for it. When Porter offered her the job, she took it.

It is probably impossible to overstate the importance of Porter Wagoner's contribution to Dolly's career in every way. He gave her her first big break, and her first national recognition. He took her away from Monument Records, where her talents were never used properly and her career was simply not getting on track, and brought her to RCA. He supervised her publicity and promotion, and he brought her to the forefront of his show far more than he had with any other female singer.

There are those who say that Dolly would have made it even without Porter, and it's hard to deny that—Dolly would have made it somehow even if the phonograph record had never been invented, and she had to walk door to door to people's houses and drop in to play. There are also those who say that Porter merely got in her way, that she would have gone even farther, even faster, if he hadn't held her back. One of these is Fred Foster of Monument Records, who said, shortly after Dolly had left the Porter Wagoner show: "I'm surprised that she hasn't broken out and crossed all the boundaries before now. I think that Porter got her timetable all fouled up or she would already be a superstar outside of country music. I imagine it took her longer to get out of that situation than she anticipated. But she's on her way now and she'll still get to the top."

Presumably, Foster's implication was that Dolly would have been a whole lot better off if she had stayed with him, but this theory can not unreasonably be dismissed as sour grapes—especially since Fred Foster's original timetable had been to try to take Dolly out of country music long before she was ready for it.

Certainly, Dolly herself would not seem to agree. She and Porter spent a long time together as music partners and close business and artistic associates, if nothing else. Their breakup—Dolly's decision to leave her partner—was a difficult and painful one, and by the end Dolly was definitely chafing under the limitations that Porter imposed on her. But she has always, even while stating their artistic differences and her need to get away, acknowledged her debt to him—"Porter did more for my career than anyone, and I'll be grateful to him for as long as I live."

Porter, very early on, made Dolly virtually a co-star on his show. Norma Jean had always been, very clearly, the girl singer on the Porter Wagoner show. But when Dolly Parton replaced her, it became Porter and Dolly. They did duets together, and recorded a number of duet albums, which Porter had never done with Norma Jean. The story goes that when she started touring with Porter, Dolly was very nervous. Porter began singing with her in rehearsals to help her overcome her jitters, and the combination clicked. A new team was born.

# DOLLY PARTON

Porter and Dolly made a strong, effective duo. To begin with, the physical impact of the two of them together was striking. Dolly, of course, is one of the most radiantly beautiful women who ever lived, a tiny butterfly for whom people have been known to break into spontaneous applause when she has done nothing more than walk into a room at a party.

Porter has an arresting, remarkable appearance in his own way: he is one of the most impressively ugly men who ever lived.

That is not meant in the slightest degree as an insult. There is only one Porter Wagoner. He is tall, skinny, with hollow, cadaverous cheeks and large, sunken eyes. He has the lips of a fat man, the jaw of a stevedore. He looks as if he could do the equivalent of cracking his knuckles with every joint in his body.

His pompadoured hair is as peroxided as Dolly's wigs, and styled every bit as improbably. It rises in front like the chest of a pouter pigeon, and swoops down in the back into a classic duck's tail. It extends down on either side into long, impeccably tailored sideburns.

Porter's outfits are sequined, rhinestoned, extravaganzas by Nudie (the tailor to rhinestone cowboys since the days of Hank Williams). It is the way country idols are supposed to dress, impossibly gaudy and yet good old boys underneath. Porter could still look at home driving a truck, but his unique looks are particularly well suited for the dramatic portraits on some of his best albums. On *Skid-Row Joe*, for example, he is stubble-bearded and dressed in rags (but still impeccably pompadoured), sitting in the gutter. And on one of the finest country album covers ever staged, for *The Cold Hard Facts of Life*, he is standing in the doorway of his tacky apartment, dressed in a blue col-

lar shirt and Windbreaker, staring aghast at his wife in the arms of another man. (The back cover is another view of the same scene, shot from behind Porter's ducktail.)

Porter and Dolly did make a marvelous combination on record, too: his cold-hard-facts voice and her otherworldly soprano mesh perfectly for romantic and dramatic ballads, his gruff stolidity and her sassiness are a delightful match on patter songs.

Porter and Dolly recorded a number of albums together during their years of partnership. Their 1971 greatest hits album, *The Best Of Porter Wagoner and Dolly Parton* (RCA LSP–4556) is a good representative collection.

Dolly has said that she left Porter because she felt strait jacketed—there was a lot that she wanted to do musically that was outside of Porter's traditional way of doing things. And that may well be true. Porter *does* have a conventional, traditional way of making music. Even comparing the solo albums that Dolly was making at the same time with the duet albums she made with Porter, the duets come out sounding more conventional.

But within this conventional, traditional style, Porter is very, very good at what he does. To begin with, he has a superb band, the Wagon Masters, that made the nucelus for his studio recording band, featuring two of the finest virtuosos in country music, electric banjo player Buck Trent and fiddler Mel McGaha. And his control over the structure of their records, working with his longtime producer Bob Ferguson, is sure and skilled.

Porter and Dolly used the common country-duet style of trading lines, and unison singing. Their unison singing is especially noteworthy. Generally, Dolly sang melody, and Porter the harmony. But in an odd aural illusion, Porter's lower tenor voice

could sound as if it were taking the melody, while Dolly's soprano appeared to be carrying the harmony. When this was added to a skillful studio mix that brought up first one voice, and then the other, as in "The Pain Of Loving You" on the *Best Of . . .* album, the sound is as smooth and satisfying a duet as you could expect to hear.

The first song that Porter and Dolly recorded—Dolly's first recording session with RCA—was Tom Paxton's folkie hit "The Last Thing On My Mind," recorded in October, 1967 and released the following month. It was not until six months later, at their third recording session, that they tried one of Dolly's compositions, the first of her recorded Gothic tales: "Jeannie's Afraid Of The Dark." Originally released as the B side of an ordinary song by fiddler Mel McGaha, "We'll Get Ahead Someday," which is more noteworthy for some nice fiddling than for Porter and Dolly's contribution, "Jeannie's Afraid Of The Dark" proved to be the strong entry on the record. Along with "The Pain Of Loving You," it is the best thing on the *Best Of . . . .* It tells the story of a little girl who is morbidly afraid of the dark, and afraid to be buried when she dies.

The rest of the album includes some nice comic exchanges between the two on "Better Move It On Home" and Dolly's "Run That By Me One More Time," and another strong Dolly Parton song, "Daddy Was an Old Time Preacher Man."

Dolly recorded so many albums, both duet and solo, during the Porter Wagoner years that there is not enough space to cover them all. Again, a good representative selection of the early years can be found on her first greatest hits album, *The Best Of Dolly Parton* (RCA LSP-4449). All but three of the songs on the album are Dolly's own compositions, and those three songs by others are the weakest

## DOLLY PARTON

on the album. First is Jimmy Rodgers' classic "Mule Skinner Blues (Blue Yodel No. 8)," a country standard that has, certainly, seen a lot worse renditions than Dolly's. But she just is not suited for the robustness of the song—it's a case of sending a girl to do a man's job. Mac Davis' soggy "In the Ghetto" (a hit for Elvis Presley), falls apart in comparison to the clean lines and precise characterizations of Dolly's own songs, and the hymn, "How Great Thou Art" is another fairly ordinary portrayal of a country hymn that virtually everybody does.

But her own songs . . . first there's "Just Because I'm a Woman," from her first solo album on RCA. While not as smooth as some of her later songs, its attack on the double standard—"My mistakes are no worse than yours just because I'm a woman— is irresistible.

The same is true for "Just the Way I Am," which initially seems to be just another bland, cute nonconformist song, but as I start finding it irresistible, also, I realize that it's happening, as with everyone who falls under Dolly's spell, I am totally unable to resist Dolly *being* Dolly, which she is in this song about chasing butterflies, leaving her housework in the middle to go out and play with children in the park, and you might as well accept her, because that's just the way she is. And as for the song—well, you might as well accept it because that's just the way she is.

The album contains "In the Good Old Days (When Times Were Bad)," "Daddy, Come and Get Me," and "Down from Dover," all discussed earlier, and two more excellent story songs.

"My Blue Ridge Mountain Boy" is a twist on the old country-boy-goes-to-the-city-leaves-good-girl-behind theme. In this song, it's the country girl who goes off to New Orleans, where it's "easy to go

wrong—the men ain't kind, like 'My Blue Ridge Mountain Boy'." With skillfully suggested details, she paints a picture of confusion, betrayal, and eventual slipping into a life of apparent prostitution, as the girl is more and more trapped in the city, more and more cut off from the good boy back home, who finally grows tired of waiting for her and marries another, so that she can never go back.

The final song, "Gypsy, Joe, and Me" is a series of deaths almost reminiscent of "Ten Little Indians" —the little dog run over on the highway, the boy friend dying of a fever, and the girl finally committing suicide to join them. Again, it's absolutely simple, and absolutely effective.

Coat Of Many Colors was a milestone in Dolly's career. In addition to the brilliant title cut, there are six other Parton originals, one of which, "Travelin' Man," is the lightest and funniest of Dolly's story songs, a charmer about a girl who sneaks out on her mother for a series of rendezvous with a traveling salesman. She finally makes plans to run off with him, only to find that the traveling man has been two-timing her with her mother, and it's her mother who actually runs off with the traveling man.

The album also has three songs by Porter, and one begins to get an idea of why Dolly eventually came to feel that Porter's influence was holding her back. The songs seem pedestrian compared to hers, although one of them, "If I Lose My Mind," which is a direct imitation of Dolly's style, does have an interesting situation—a woman who is afraid she has been driven insane by her husband's trying to force her to participate in wife swapping ("He made me watch him love another woman, and he tried to make me love another man").

And a later album, *Dolly Parton Sings "My Favorite Songwriter, Porter Wagoner"* (RCA LSP-4572) bears this out even more clearly. The liner notes by Dolly on the back of the album proclaim her "so very, very proud of this album, because I think the songs in it are some of the greatest songs I have ever heard and certainly the greatest I have ever sung," but they aren't. They range from mediocre to bad.

*My Tennessee Mountain Home*, containing the previously released "In the Good Old Days (When Times Were Bad)," plus new songs on the theme of real or imagined childhood reminiscences came out the next year. The album is helped immeasurably by the brilliant backup work of Porter's band, especially Buck Trent and Mel McGaha; it is also helped considerably by not having any of Porter's songs on it.

By this time Dolly's reputation was really starting to grow, as was the reputation of country music. Other performers, including pop stars like Emmylou Harris and Linda Ronstadt, were starting to record her songs, and she was beginning to come to the attention of an audience outside of the world of country music.

Around this time, Dolly must have begun to reconsider her association with Porter.

Were Dolly and Porter lovers?

Dolly says no. "It was a very unique relationship. Porter and me are a lot alike. Our music bound us close together. We had as much respect for each other as love . . . but that don't mean we were lovers."

It was certainly widely assumed that they were lovers, by fellow performers as well as fans. Dolly counters that the same assumption was made about

every girl singer that Porter worked with—Porter
has always been known as the kind of good old
boy who liked his women, and who fell hard for
them. His friends tend to automatically toss "trouble
with a woman" into the list of reasons when
Porter falls apart.

But Dolly and Porter didn't do all that much to
dispel the rumors. Certainly the titles of their duet
albums could only add grist to the mill: *Just Between
You and Me* ... *Just the Two of Us* ... *Always,
Always* ... *The Right Combination* ... *We
Found It* .. *Two of a Kind* ... *Together Always* ...
*Love and Music.*

And their habit of giving each other little gifts
didn't do anything to nip the rumors in the bud,
either. Among the little gifts that Porter gave Dolly
were five diamond rings, two Cadillacs, and two
diamond necklaces. Among the little gifts that
Dolly gave Porter was a half interest in Owepar,
her music publishing firm.

Still, album covers are just made-up publicity,
and let's assume they weren't lovers. Nothing more
than gossip says they were; Dolly says absolutely
no, and are you going to look into those wide,
long-lashed, innocent blue-green eyes and dispute
it?

But there doesn't seem to be much doubt in anyone's
mind that Porter, for his part, was totally
smitten with Dolly, and that it came as a tremendous
blow to him when she decided to go it alone.

Porter never really imagined that Dolly would
leave him, his friends say. One gets the impression
that he came to think of their future in much
the same way that married couples plan theirs—
"he used to talk of what they'd be doing when
they got tired of the road," in the words of one
associate.

And while the full story of the breakup has never

been told by either side, enough has emerged from allusions that both have made, plus whatever friends have been able or willing to fill in, to make it apparent that there were a number of intense and difficult scenes between them, a lot of threats, a lot of pain, until finally Dolly was able to convince Porter that she was going to leave whether he liked it or not. The only question, then, was whether or not the split would be friendly, in which case they could continue at least some part of their work association, or whether Dolly would leave him completely.

Porter bowed to the inevitable. He held a press conference, and made the announcement. He had decided that it was time for Dolly to go out on her own, and she would be leaving his show to tour with her own group. But he would still be producing her records.

Over the next couple of years, during the period in which she was half free from Porter and half connected to him, Dolly released four albums: *Jolene* (RCA APL1-0473), *Love Is Like a Butterfly* (RCA APL1-0712), *The Bargain Store* (RCA APL1-0950), and *Dolly (The Seeker/We Used To)* (RCA APL1-1221.)

*Jolene* follows the structure of a conventional, old-fashioned sort of album—that is, two songs obviously designed to be released as singles, and promoted toward the country charts (at least), plus a bunch of other songs that were more or less thrown together to fill out an album. All but two of the songs were written by Dolly; two songs on the album are lifted from earlier Parton records.

This is not the most striking of Dolly's efforts. Its two hits, "Jolene" and "I Will Always Love You" are both lacking in the qualities that make a Parton song so special and distinctive: the deceptively simple emotional wallop, the strong story line, the deeply personal involvement, genuinely autobiographical or not—"She has the ability to put herself into a situation and write about it," as Porter described her talent. "She hasn't personally experienced in any form many of the situations she writes about, but yet she can imagine those experiences in such great detail that she can write songs about them, great songs."

That ability gets stretched a little thin in "Jolene." There is a situation—a plain, ordinary woman whose home is threatened by an auburn-haired temptress who has captured the infatuation of the singer's man. She has no hope of holding on to him by her own resources, no hope of his being strong enough to resist this overwhelming temptation; her only hope is a plea to Jolene to take pity on her, woman to woman, and leave the poor schlump alone. It's not a bad song, but it can't match the insights and character delineation of Dolly's great ones.

Perhaps writing about a woman who is so completely helpless is more of a leap of imagination than Dolly can make, or perhaps it's a subject that just doesn't sit well with her. Perhaps it should not come as any kind of a surprise that the one other singer who has recorded "Jolene" is Olivia Newton-John.

"I Will Always Love You," on the other hand, *is* a bad song. It is about as imaginative in theme and treatment as the title would indicate. It's been recorded on a recent album by Linda Ronstadt, and it's a bad song when she does it, too.

The rest of the album can be passed over briefly. Up-tempo numbers like "River Of Happiness" only point up how much better the old sound was, with Porter's band backing her up. The blandest tune on *My Tennessee Mountain Home*, with Buck Trent and Mel McGaha helping out, is sprightlier than the liveliest song on *Jolene*. There is the beginning of an experiment with a sort of blues style in "Living on Memories of You," which is interesting, but the experiment is better brought to fruition on the next album with "Love is Like a Butterfly."

Actually, the very best song on the album *Jolene* is one that was lifted from *Coat Of Many Colors*: "Early Morning Breeze."

"Early Morning Breeze" has a lovely, Appalachian/folkish melody, and simple lyric that expresses a pure wonderment at the beauty of nature:

> Rainbow-colored meadow kissed with early
> morning sun
> The aster and the daisy and the wild geranium
> Drops of morning dew still linger on the iris
> leaves
> In the meadow where I'm walking in the early
> morning breeze.

*Love Is Like A Butterfly* follows much the same format, except that it has only one hit, the title cut. But it's a much better album.

"Love Is Like A Butterfly"—the song—is a worthy lead piece for the album. It is a little precocious, if you want to carp, and Dolly is probably the only singer who could make it work at all (no one else has tried to cover it). But her butterfly-like delivery, the delicate, folkish melody and almost too-pretty words just flutter right along, into your memory and into your heart.

There's nothing else on the first side of the album that's worth commenting on at all—except that "Take Me Back," a terrible copy of the themes of "My Tennessee Mountain Home," marks the historic first known use of the word "bosom" in a Dolly Parton Song.

Some of the songs on *Love Is Like A Butterfly* run the danger of reminding the listener of some-

thing else—another song on the same theme that was better; and that is really a kiss of death for any song.

"Blackie, Kentucky," is a rehash of "My Blue Ridge Mountain Boy," with overtones of Porter's classic "Green, Green Grass of Home": A young woman from a poor coal mining family leaves home to go to the city and marry a rich snob; there she finds herself a prisoner, a bird in a gilded cage. The only way she can ever go back home is to kill herself, and leave a note requesting that she be buried in the family plot back in good old Blackie, Kentucky.

"You're the One Who Taught Me How to Swing" is strongly reminiscent of Tammy Wynette's hit, "Your Good Girl's Gonna Go Bad," the story of the nice girl who is being forced—or in the case of Dolly's song, has been forced—into a life of being a bad girl. Dolly's song adds little to the genre—and for prurient references to swinging, Porter's "If I Lose My Mind" is a lot more dishonorably rewarding.

But halfway through the second side of the album, things really start to pick up. Dolly romps and stomps through a rousing version of the old Porter Wagoner foot-stomping classic, "Highway Headin' South." All the songs on this album are by either Dolly or Porter; and while Dolly may have been chafing under what she saw as the strait jacket of Porter Wagoner-style music, she picked a winner in this one. It's good-time music at its best.

Then, in "Once Upon a Memory," Dolly and producer Bob Ferguson do some of the experimenting with different musical styles that Dolly had been saying she wanted to do. "Once Upon a Memory" begins with a rhythm-and-blues style guitar riff, and builds into an Elvis-orchestral, blues-based arrangement backing up Dolly's stirring, Elvis-influenced rhythm-and-blues vocal.

Dolly proves she can do it. She has that country soul, and she has the musical versatility. The only thing about the whole project that is less than completely satisfactory is the stiltedness of the title phrase that serves as the song's hook, "Once Upon a Memory."

Finally, there's "Sacred Memories," which starts out threatening to be yet another mom and dad's waltz of sentimentality about the past, but quickly turns out to be, instead, a stirring tribute to the old mountain gospel songs like "I Can't Feel at Home in the World Any More," "If We Ever Meet Again," and "Power in the Blood." "Sacred Memories" combines a fine, contemporary arrangement with great old gospel vocal harmonies, and it skillfully threads the music and lyrics of the old spirituals into a new song that is at once a medley and a tight, unified composition in its own right.

*The Bargain Store* is the best album to come out of this period, a delight from beginning to end. Once again, it mostly features songs by Dolly, with one composition by Porter and one from a new source, country star Merle Haggard. (Hag returned the compliment, recording one of Dolly's songs from this album, "Kentucky Gambler.")

*The Bargain Store* is the first album of Dolly's on which Porter Wagoner is credited as producer—or rather, he shares the production credit with Bob Ferguson, long-time producer for both Porter and Dolly. And listening to the album, frankly, makes one wonder just what it was that Dolly was thinking when she decided that she was stifled by Porter's production ideas, because the work on this album is flawless, from the pacing and balance of the songs, to the details that make even the less exciting songs on the album worth listening

to—the terrific guitar break on "The Only Hand You'll Ever Need to Hold" to subtle filling by the backup vocalists on Porter's tune, "Love to Remember."

There just aren't any low points on this album, but here are some of the high points:

"The Bargain Store." Amazingly, this poignant song of courage, hope, and retrieved scraps of self-respect in a torn and battered life was banned on many country stations for suggestive lyrics. Dolly was justifiably upset by the lewdness that in this case, was certainly in the mind of the beholder. She told Chet Flippo:

"When I said the bargain store is open, come inside, I just meant my *life* is open, come into my life, so I wasn't even thinkin' of it as a dirty thing ... I had probably been kicked around some. Not by my husband... but you know, me and Porter, we just kind of said things, hurt each other's feelings and... trampled on territory that was real sensitive, cut each other about songs."

If Dolly and Porter were hurting each other then, they must have both used their pain to best effect on this one.

"The Bargain Store" is a woman's plea, and a statement of who she is. As Dolly explains it, it "means I have been in love before and kicked around and had my head and by heart broke, my cherry stole, but I can grow *another* one if that's what you want."

"Kentucky Gambler" is a story song, unusual for Dolly in that it's about a man. The story—a gambler leaves his family in Kentucky to follow his luck, hits it big for a while and then goes bust, loses his wife and family in the process—is heavily moralistic, but delivered with a light, up-tempo, easy style that puts the moralizing in perspective. It's full of strong, simple rhymes, Dolly's usual skill

at presenting a story in straightforward, economical language leavened with some startlingly poetic lines like "Reno dreams fade into neon embers," and wonderful little vocal tricks.

"When I'm Gone" is rousing, feisty, energetic, fun. "You'll Always Be Special to Me" is the Merle Haggard song, and his rough, masculine sincerity is an effective contrast to her pure, feminine sincerity. "He Would Know" (described earlier), the song about temptation on the road and the love of a good man at home, is on this album. And the final song is "I'll Never Forget," another haunting folkie melody and a simple, touching love lyric.

*Dolly (The Seeker/We Used To)* is probably best described in these words by Dolly herself, from the jacket of the album:

"I write songs about many subjects. I love to write songs, and love is one of my favorite subjects to write about. I have included in this album some of my favorite love songs, and I hope they will become some of your favorites."

Love, Dolly. And that's the album. It's a little more monochromatic than most of her other albums, but it's a perfectly pleasant collection of love songs. It could find a home next to anyone's Barbra Streisand and Barry Manilow records, and is likely to be the old Dolly record which would appeal most to new Dolly fans. The songs are about different shades of love working and love not working, and one's favorites on it would most likely be in line with the relative success or failure of one's love life at the time.

The one exception is "The Seeker," a spiritual number which is different from everything one expects of a country gospel song. Instead of being celebratory and sanctified, it is reflective, even a little cautious.

## DOLLY PARTON

"I know there is a God," Dolly told Chet Flippo, discussing "The Seeker," "... but I'm one of the world's sinners. I think I'm a vanilla sinner—too bad to be good and too good to be bad ... it wouldn't be *all* that hard to be good but I just don't know that I *want* to be ... I just couldn't decide whether I wanted to be a Christian or not ... So I wrote that out of a heavy heart. Because I certainly am *not* a Christian. I will try some of *anything*, I mean I will."

# 12

Those two years were a period of success, growth, and frustration in the life of Dolly Parton.

The success was in the rising, widespread popularity that she was achieving. Her records were reaching larger and larger audiences. She won the Country Music Association's Female Vocalist of the Year award for the first time in 1975, then again in 1976. She was written up in *Rolling Stone* for the first time. Her songs were being picked up and recorded by all sorts of performers, pop stars as well as country. She had her own syndicated television show, out of Nashville.

Her growth was in taking more and more control of her own career. She had her own band now, for the first time, Dolly Parton's Traveling Family Band, made up of members of her own family. She was wearing the costumes she wanted to wear on stage, not what Porter thought would suit the decor of his show the best. She was organizing her own tours, and playing to audiences that had come to see *her*.

## DOLLY PARTON

The frustration had two different sources. The first was that some of her own decisions were turning out to be not the best. But that wasn't so bad—everyone makes mistakes, and she was learning from hers. It was the second source of frustration that really ate away at her—that she was still not in control the way she wanted to be. She still felt stifled, stifled by Porter, stifled by Nashville. There were things she wanted to do, things that she sensed would be right for her, and she wasn't able to do them. She has told friends that those two years were the most miserable years of her life.

Porter was still helping Dolly then, helping her perhaps more than she really wanted to be helped. Or, perhaps it would be closer to the truth to say that the ways in which Porter was helping Dolly were tying more strings to her than she could be comfortable with. When Dolly went to Porter for advice on organizational problems, he responded by turning over his own manager, Don Warden, to her.

This was no small gesture for Porter to make. Warden had been with him for twenty-two years, and when Porter said that it would take "three men to replace him in my organization," there is no doubt but that he meant exactly what he said. It was an act of great generosity—a loving act, even —and yet, both Dolly and Porter must have been very much aware of its implications. It meant that Dolly's management, decisions that would be made regarding the direction of her career, what she would and would not be doing, what goals she would and would not be striving for, would all be in the hands of a capable and efficient man who thought exactly like Porter.

It meant that the man who would be closest to her in her business life would be a man who, by

# DOLLY PARTON

habit and inclination, had a deep and abiding loyalty to Porter Wagoner.

In the short run, Warden may have helped Dolly. In the long run—and the long run, in this case, was not much longer than the short run—it probably simply confirmed her feeling that she had to get away from Porter. Only a couple of months later, she went to the top brass at RCA, and told them she wanted to get out of her deal with Porter.

Porter was supposed to produce three more albums for her. He had produced only one of the three, but RCA went along with Dolly. Porter was out. And at the same time, Dolly dropped Don Warden, and replaced him with the Hollywood firm, Katz, Gallin, and Cleary.

Dolly's last record with Porter was *All I Can Do*, "Produced by 'Porter and Dolly'," the credit reads, which was still too much Porter to suit Dolly. It's a fine album with some first-rate songs by Dolly, including "All I Can Do," "Shattered Image," "Preacher Tom," and "Hey, Lucky Lady." Another Merle Haggard tune, "Life's Like Poetry," is on the album, and a haunting if cryptic ballad by Dolly's new friend, Emmylou Harris, called "Boulder to Birmingham." It's a much more varied album than its predecessor.

One other Porter-produced album, a duet, is completed but has never been released by RCA, and will not be in the foreseeable future. Porter and Dolly is not the image that either RCA or Katz, Gallin, Cleary and Parton want to promote.

Porter was understandably hurt. "I guess they thought our duets were too country for her," he told *Music City News*. "I think it was a huge mistake. I think the duets were a big part of her career, and I think *I* was a big part of her career."

Porter is certainly not alone in his feelings. "Porter is a fantastic musician," says Nashville studio musician Charlie Chappelear. "He did a lot of great stuff with Dolly. He was able to capture her essence, a pure country, from-out-of-the-mountains type sound. He really captured her true flavor, and he surrounded it, and he never subtracted from it, and he didn't add to it—he was very careful in that respect. Of course, when she decided to get more progressive, Porter's tracks seemed far behind her ... only history will tell if that was a good move or a bad move."

If breaking with Porter was like firing a member of her own family, then Porter didn't have to feel like the Lone Ranger. Because Dolly did that, too. In fact, she fired her whole family, or at least her whole Family Band. It had been a cute idea, but they weren't going to be able to give her the sound she wanted. Besides, adding family squabbles to musical problems was proving to be more trouble than it was worth. Dolly started to put together a new band, made up of top musicians.

"Dolly is fantastic to work with, for a musician," says Clyde Brooks, the original drummer in that new band. "She has the ability to inspire her musicians to greater heights—and when the musicians get going, she can stay with them. A lot of singers can't do that—the musicians really start cooking, and the singer just drops out. But Dolly is always right there."

So she needed musicians who could keep up with *her*. And this was to be the band with which she was going to make the big push for her new career, so a lot of planning went into the forming of it.

Charlie Chappelear was one of the musicians who was involved in creating that band. He had joined Dolly at the end of the Traveling Family

# DOLLY PARTON

Band days, and became the first band leader of the second band, which was to be called Gypsy Fever.

"We needed a band that would be capable of doing this new album, *New Harvest . . . First Gathering*," Chappelear recalls, "a band that could carry her in her pop direction. Also, musicians that were capable of doing her television show, which we were also saddled with at the time (Dolly had signed to do a syndicated music show, similar to Porter's, based in Nashville), and musicians who not only were good enough to do all that, but would be free to travel and do the concerts."

That's a tall order, and one that wouldn't normally be necessary for one group of musicians. Most Nashville stars have musicians that they tour with, but for their albums they fall back on the great studio musicians that Nashville is full of. But Dolly's original concept at this time was to form a group —"Sort of like Fleetwood Mac or Wings," Chappelear describes it. "A group that produces themselves. She didn't want to be left alone to make all the creative decisions."

But Dolly must have had very mixed feelings on that score. After all, she had left Porter in good part because she wasn't getting the control over her recordings that she wanted; and whatever her original concept, things began more and more to settle on her.

"Dolly had told me that Porter had treated his musicians like a dictator," says Chappelear. "She wanted to get away from that and treat everybody real nice . . . But as it developed, she made the days with Porter seem like the Athenian Democracy compared with Czarist Russia."

Dolly described *New Harvest . . . First Gathering* to Chet Flippo as "a new freedom for me, just total

self-expression and daring to be brave, just to see music the way I totally feel it."

"She wanted to get the music to come out the way she heard it inside," says Clyde Brooks. "She's an intuitive producer. I just remember a lot of time in the studio, working over and over until we got it the way she wanted it."

And what did they get? *New Harvest . . . First Gathering* is an interesting album, a carefully planned album. It has lots of different kinds of music on it, new types of songs, something for all tastes. It has one foot in country, one foot in pop, and yet both feet are planted firmly on the ground of the territory that they're in. The dual voice seems different, not the result of confusion.

And yet, perhaps even more than the albums that preceded it, *New Harvest . . . First Gathering* is dominated by one song, the marvelous "Light of a Clear Blue Morning."

"Light of a Clear Blue Morning" is an anthem of liberation, of independence, of realizing one's own potential. It is Dolly's song, it is a woman's song, it is anybody's song, anybody beginning to feel the courage to seize the moment and begin to lead her, or his, own life: "I've been like a captured eagle . . . an eagle's born to fly, Now that I've won my freedom, Like an eagle, I am eager for the sky."

# DOLLY PARTON

"Applejack" is the real country song on the album—Dolly's bow to old Nashville, and to her past. The roster of backup singers sounds like a list of charter members of the Country Music Hall of Fame—Roy Acuff, Ernest Tubb, Wilma Lee and Stoney Cooper, Kittye Wells, Minnie Pearl, etc.—plus Porter's gift manager, Don Warden, and her old producer, Bob Ferguson.

There are two soul classics given a pop treatment on the album—the Temptations' "My Girl" ("My Love" in Dolly's version), and Jackie Wilson's "Higher and Higher." That's certainly a new concept for her, and a not uninteresting one. But perhaps trying to turn these two songs into vehicles for a country soprano trying to go pop is a little more of a strain than they can support.

There is a sense of strain, of trying a little too hard throughout the album. It's very much present in "You Are," which includes a spoken bridge.

Dolly's speaking voice in earlier songs like "The Letter" from *My Tennessee Mountain Home* (or, for that matter, later songs like "Me and Little Andy"), is something akin to a national treasure. Just answering questions at a press conference, she can speak in a voice described by writer Carla Sweet as: "You could dance to it." But on "You Are," the music is choked out of it when she presses too hard for dramatic heaviness.

On "There"—a sort of spiritual, though not exactly a country spiritual—there's a fascinating experiment, in that the chorus, "Take me there—won't you take me there," is sung alternately by adults' and children's voices. Again, though, there's a sense of trying a little too hard for a striking effect.

But if these things miss, they don't miss by much. Maybe they don't miss at all. "There" is quite lovely. "Where Beauty Lives in Memory" is a fas-

cinating psychological insight in the form of a story song. And "Light of a Clear Blue Morning" is something special.

Dolly has admitted that perhaps she overproduced *New Harvest*, fearing that she might never get a chance to produce again, and wanting to try everything she had on her mind. But she told Alanna Nash, in her *Country Music* magazine interview:

"Even if *New Harvest . . . First Gathering* doesn't sell a nickel's worth, it will always be my special album, because it was the first time in my whole life I got to do something totally on my own. In terms of fulfillment, it's one of the greatest things of my life."

 Dolly had received movie offers before, for low-budget country music films, all of which she had turned down. They weren't what she wanted, and she wasn't ready. But she had her sights on a movie career, and on becoming a sex symbol, as part of her path to superstardom.

One plan she considered and discussed with intimates was following up *New Harvest* with an album which would feature the songs of Bill Monroe, and which she could then title *Monroe*, and use as the cover photo the famous Marilyn Monroe pose from *The Seven Year Itch*, skirts billowing around her upper thighs—naturally, with Dolly taking the Marilyn part.

But Dolly did not have to make her overtures in such a roundabout way. As with so many of her little-girl heroines in her songs, the angels came and took her away. Only these angels were emissaries from the City of Angels, Los Angeles. Their names were Katz, Gallin and Cleary, and they took Dolly with them to their home among the stars.

# DOLLY PARTON

Charlie Chappelear, who has very definite reservations about the artistic development of this stage of Dolly's career, says, "I think her management company is a great company. If I ever had any ambitions to be a superstar, I wouldn't mind signing up with them."

They put Dolly on a road right up to the top. They got her nationwide television exposure as a personality on the Johnny Carson show, and *Hollywood Squares*. They refused to allow her to be interviewed for an *Esquire* article on Dolly, Tammy Wynette, and Loretta Lynn, "the three queens of country music," because "we don't want her lumped in with those country singers." They made sure, on the other hand, that her more lucrative (though certainly genuine) friendships with pop stars Linda Ronstadt and Emmylou Harris were quite well known.

And when everyone knew who she was, they brought out her new album.

*Here You Come Again* was recorded in Los Angeles, using all Los Angeles musicians, and a Los Angeles producer, Gary Klein, who has also produced Barbra Streisand. The cover opens up double to reveal, on the inside, a soft-focus, dreamy portrait of Dolly, so grainy as to give the effect of a pointillist painting. The outside cover, front and back, is a shiny, hard-edged series of photographs of Dolly that look—except for what becomes the genuinely minor detail that she's fully clothed—like a photo spread for *Playboy*. The other interesting point about this album is that it has nothing at all on it that even comes close to being a country song.

*Here You Come Again* went platinum, that is, it sold over a million units, and it's hard to argue with success. I know some perfectly nice people who like it, and lots and lots of perfectly nice people whom I don't know, also like it. It has songs on it by Barry Mann and Cynthia Weil, Bobby Goldsboro, and John Sebastian, as well as a couple of songs by Dolly. It doesn't sound like an album by the woman who made "Light of a Clear Blue Morning" or "My Tennessee Mountain Home." It doesn't have much feeling. But it sure does go down smooth.

Dolly explained the album to Martha Hume as "a special event. I was purposely tryin' to do somethin' to get myself established in the other field of music. And I knew that what I'd done in the past wasn't what I needed to fill that gap. So I just agreed, on the advice of my manager, to let them do the album, which they did. And it was platinum and I can't argue with success."

"But," she goes on, "that don't mean that there aren't other ways to be successful. I even expect I'll go back to producin' my own, eventually."

She has co-produced her current album, *Heartbreaker*, with Gary Klein. But in all likelihood, producing will have to wait a while on the demands of superstardom. She is planning—although the project seems to keep running into snags—the first all-woman super session, with Linda Ronstadt. She is still writing. Emmylou Harris has recorded a new Parton song, "To Daddy," which is a stunner, a look at the familiar mama-and-daddy theme of earlier Parton songs from a penetrating and profoundly feminist new perspective. Emmylou has praised Dolly's genius as a songwriter. "I've never seen anyone so spontaneously creative," she told Lani Rogers (*Songwriter's Review*, June/July, 1978). "I've watched Dolly writing one song while she's singing another." And Linda, for her part, has credited Dolly for teaching her how to be a woman.

And in mid-1978, Dolly signed a three-picture deal with 20th Century Fox.

# 14

This is Dolly on the brink of a new career, a new life, in her own words, from a press conference in Madison, Wisconsin, June 29, 1978:

"I don't think [going pop] was a mistake. I think people understand I'm just trying to do everything I'm capable of doing, as far as music goes, 'cause that's how I make my living. I hope to win more fans, and keep the fans I already have—or at least, to win back the fans I might have lost through what I do in the future. I'm real happy. I have my organization in real good order, I'm making money for the first time, seeing some results from my ole hard work, and I'll just keep trying to do the best I can with it.

"Staying power in this business is knowing what kind of show you should do, that's best suited to your type of personality and talent, being always aware of what you can do to improve, and knowing your audience and what it is they really want to hear, country or middle of the road. To stay there, you have to have talent, but it takes a lot of hard work, backbone, and the guts to try different things. You have to please yourself and the audience.

"I never felt hemmed in by country music. Don't get me wrong; I love country music—It's my first love, it always was, and it always will be. But I just did not want to feel like I was not allowed to do other things. We're all country at heart. Country just means a feeling, getting down to real stories, things that people can relate to. You can be country and live in the city, and vice versa. So I am just a country girl who wanted to go to town.

"I'm happier now. I don't mind the pressure [of success] because I know that responsibility goes along with any job, whether it's a waitress or a secretary or the head of a company. I deal with the pressure by trying to stay in the areas that I know best. I feel better now because I've found new management, people that really do know what to do, and where to place my talent and help me carry out my ideas. I have a good band now, good lighting, and I have a lot of good fans— country, and some others that I've won in the past year-and-a-half. I'm happier now than I've ever been, because it makes you feel good to see something you've worked at so hard becoming successful. It makes you feel like you were right, no matter how hard people sometimes want to make you feel you've done the wrong thing.

"For the last two years I've been on the road about two-hundred days a year. Before that, I usually worked about eight to ten days a month. I hope to get back to that, but I've felt it was really important to take my music to the audience, so that the country fans can see that I'm still the Dolly they always knew, and so that the new fans can see that there is a person under the gaude and all the outrageous costumes, a person with love for my music, and love for the audience, and a talent under all the hair.

"When I started going on the road two-hundred days a year, Carl started spending a lot of time with me. He did see me in concert, and he got real emotional about it. He really liked it. I was better than he thought I was. I guess he didn't know what I could do, because he just always knew me as the person that he loved, and he knew me in a way that no one else ever will. I guess he was just afraid I would not do well, and he was glad to see that at least I had control of what it is that I do.

"I just signed a deal to do three movies for 20th Century Fox. I never had thought that much about the movies, but I had always wanted to try some of everything that had to do with entertainment, and that's another outlet for my music. I'll be able to write the songs for the movies. I hope one of them will be a comedy, and maybe the other will be more serious, and one of the movies, I hope, will be my life story. I don't look to be singing in every movie . . . most likely, the songs I write will be in the background, as usual movies go, for themes, and whatever.

"I think it's fun doing the Johnny Carson show, and I'm used to the jokes he makes—I make as many jokes about myself, now, as other people. At first, I didn't quite know how to take the jokes. I didn't know if they were meant to be insults, or if I should be embarrassed, or whatever. But . . . if I'm gonna look like this, I might as well have fun with it, too.

"Before all the publicity started, I had a pretty large following in what they called underground circles. People knew I was a writer and a singer before they really knew how I looked. People were buying my albums, recording my songs. The country fans knew I was a writer, and they had ac-

cepted the fact that I had an outrageous image. Now, people that didn't know before just have to get over the shock of my image before they can get real serious about my music, which is sad, because the whole purpose of the image was a gimmick to catch their attention, and then to let them know there was a person underneath it that did sing, and write songs, and was very serious about her music. I think soon, though everybody'll be over the shock of what I look like, and get back to the music. That's what I'm hoping for.

"I may change my image ... I might even get more outrageous. I'll know when the time comes ... I don't intend to change my image right now. You can overcome an image, or whatever you have to, if you have something more to offer.

"Emmylou Harris and Linda Ronstadt and I did get in the studio last winter, and we were hoping that we could do an album in a month, which was the only time the three of us had. But it's almost impossible to do any kind of an album, especially something that special, with three artists like us, and we got involved, and we didn't get finished. We did record several songs, but there were several that we didn't want to be on the album. We're still discussing it, but we all had to go back to work. We don't know when it'll come out. There's a lot of pressure being put on the project, because there's three different artists, with three different managements, three different labels, and you'd be surprised how many business things can come up.

"We were all fired up to do it, and to do a tour. We had hoped we would be able to do some touring this summer. But until the album comes out, and until we know exactly what we're doing with the album, we'll have to wait before we schedule any tours. There's no point in doing the tours until the album is out.

## DOLLY PARTON

"I worked in a show about two weeks ago with Linda and the Beach Boys, and that was the first time I had played to a rock audience. I thought, well, with a country person, they might not accept us too well, but they really liked us, and my show went over as good as the others—and I didn't even know if some of them even knew who I was. So it could be done—the three of us could tour together, and would work out. It wasn't a matter of having to follow someone, people don't usually compare you. People know what you do, and they expect to hear your songs. I went back out with Linda on that show and did a couple of songs.

"There is a chance that the album might be scratched altogether. There always is, when you're doing big business with labels, and managers, and artists. We hope that won't happen. But there is that possibility. But I think that it's such a special project that we will find a way to work out the business problems, and . . . you know, what type of songs we want to do, what type of album it should be. We're still trying to decide between ourselves what the album actually should sound like, and with three different people, you'll get three different ideas. Maybe it'll just be an acoustic album, old-timey songs, or a variety of some country, some rock, some folk. But that's the thing we're still involved in, trying to work that out.

"I don't regard Stella [Parton, her sister] as competition, I regard her as my sister, that's doing quite well, and that I'm very proud of. In fact, we have other brothers and sisters that are recording now, and you'll probably be seeing all kinds of Partons, if you can stand it."

15

Where does Dolly go from here? For someone with her talent, her ambition, and her remarkable physical presence, the possibilities are almost limitless. She could be the biggest woman star in the music business, ever.

She could be the Elvis Presley of the 1980s.

The parallels are all there. Like Elvis, she has burst out of Southern genre music and onto the nationwide scene, into the big time, leaving a hole in the fabric of conventional expectations so wide that others are following. In Elvis' wake, a generation of country boys like Carl Perkins and Jerry Lee Lewis, Conway Twitty and Charlie Rich, became rock-and-rollers. When the rockabilly boom went bust, they all wandered back into the country, but Elvis remained King. Of everything.

Dolly is sparking the same kind of phenomenon. "I think it's great," says Clyde Brooks of Dolly's new direction. "Everyone down here is going to have to start broadening their style. And Dolly is showing the way."

## DOLLY PARTON

After Dolly, we've seen the pop charts invaded by songs like Crystal Gayle's "Don't It Make My Brown Eyes Blue"—and while Dolly's Hollywood television stints were condemned by the Nashville Old Guard when she started, today Loretta Lynn, Crystal's big sister and so pure-country that she admits to having trouble writing her own name, is now doing guest shots on *Hollywood Squares*. All of that may be just another fad, and nobody expects Loretta Lynn to be the next Paul Lynde—but when it fades, don't bet on Dolly fading with it. Don't be surprised if she's still right up there, like Elvis.

The Queen. Of everything.

Dolly is heading for Hollywood now, like Elvis before her. Elvis spent close to twenty years in Hollywood, making one awful film after another, every one of which made huge profits and increased his popularity. No one knows what kinds of movies Dolly will be making—but a current rumor has her co-starring with Arnold Schwarzenegger, the former Mr. Universe.

Well, for all that Elvis did, he was still the King. His old fans, who loved "Mystery Train" and "Heartbreak Hotel," may have hated *Viva Las Vegas* or *Paradise—Hawaiian Style* or *In the Ghetto*, but they could never quite bring themselves to dismiss or abandon him.

So it would not be a good idea, even for an old country purist like me, to sell Dolly short. Who's to say she can't do it all? Like Elvis, maybe she'll just keep on growing bigger—in popularity, that is. Certainly no one would wish for her to lose her figure the way Elvis did. Maybe she'll do everything she says she wants to do—keep all her old fans, and add more and more new ones.

I hope so. It would be exciting to see a woman do it. It would be exciting to see *Dolly* do it. But

## DOLLY PARTON

I can't help but suspect that twenty years from now, people will be saying—as with Elvis—that her best and most exciting work was her early work, before she got super-big and went Hollywood. Songs like "Coat of Many Colors," and "The Bargain Store," and "Down from Dover," and "The Letter":

> ... and I don't want you to worry about me getting in trouble ... cause I'll be good, just like I promised you I would ... tell everybody I said hello ... cause I sure do miss you, and I love you an awful lot. Love, Dolly.

THE GREENHOUSE
DANCE ENSEMBLE

NATALIE RICHMAN
BEVERLY BROWN
CAROL CONWAY
NADA REAGAN
ROBERT YOHN
LILLO WAY

THE          FMANN
CO
OF THE          R
1395 LEX  GTON AV  NY N  10028

# DISCOGRAPHY

# DOLLY PARTON

## Discount Dolly

These are records that have been put out on low-priced labels, and represent Dolly at the beginning of her career. The first is very early, masters that Dolly made while she was still struggling, still trying to find her voice. It has only one side devoted to Dolly Parton, another singer on the flip. It's not recommended. The other two are early RCA albums that are available now on RCA budget labels. They sell for about $2.50 each, and they're well worth it, each of them featuring some of Dolly's best songs.

## Dolly Parton Sings
*Alshire 5-5351*

It Wasn't God That Made Honky Tonk Angels
Making Believe
Letter to Heaven
Release Me
Little Blossom
Two Little Orphans

## Just Because I'm a Woman
*Camden 7017*

Mule Skinner Blues
She Never Met a Man She Didn't Like
Big Wind
Try Being Lonely
Love Isn't Free
D-I-V-O-R-C-E
The Fire's Still Burning
Daddy
Just Because I'm a Woman

## Mine
*Pickwick ACL-0307*

Mine
Chas

## DOLLY PARTON

When Possession Gets Too Strong
I'm Doing This for Your Sake
But You Loved Me Then
Don't Let It Trouble Your Mind
More Than Their Share
Mama Say a Prayer
Down from Dover

There are so many Dolly Parton albums, from her earliest country years up through the present, that a complete discography would be extremely space-consuming. The following is a list of Dolly's records, with more detailed information on the ones still easily available, or of special interest. A consumer note—virtually all of the early albums are short—they tend to run less than thirteen minutes per side. It isn't until Dolly's first production on her own, *New Harvest . . . First Gathering*, that the records begin to run over fifteen or sixteen minutes a side, the length that pop and rock fans are more used to. And yes, there are two albums called *The Best of Dolly Parton*, without so much as Volume I or Volume II to distinguish them.

### In the Beginning
*Monument MG 7623*
*Producer: Fred Foster*

Dumb Blonde
Fuel to the Flame
The Little Things
The Company You Keep
Why, Why, Why
Somethin' Fishy
Put It Off Until Tomorrow
I'm in No Condition
As Long As I Love
Too Lonely Too Long

## DOLLY PARTON

**In the Good Old Days (When Times Were Bad)**
*RCA LSP-4099*

**My Blue Ridge Mountain Boy**
*RCA LSP-4188*

**The Fairest of Them All**
*RCA LSP-4288*

**A Real Live Dolly**
*RCA LSP-4387*
*(A live album, with guest appearance by Porter Wagoner)*

**Golden Streets of Glory**
*RCA LSP-4398*

**The Best of Dolly Parton**
*RCA LSP-4449*
*Producer: Bob Ferguson*

Mule Skinner Blues (Blue Yodel No. 8)
Down from Dover
My Blue Ridge Mountain Boy
In the Good Old Days
Gypsy, Joe and Me
In the Ghetto
Just Because I'm a Woman
Daddy Come and Get Me
How Great Thou Art
Just the Way I Am

**Joshua**
*RCA LSP-4507*

**Coat of Many Colors**
*RCA LSP-4603*
*Producer: Bob Ferguson*

Coat of Many Colors
Traveling Man
My Blue Tears

## DOLLY PARTON

If I Lose My Mind
The Mystery of the Mystery
She Never Met a Man
Early Morning Breeze
The Way I See You
Here I Am
A Better Place to Live

**Touch Your Woman**
*RCA LSP-4686*

**Dolly Parton Sings "My Favorite Songwriter, Porter Wagoner"**
*RCA LSP-4761*
*Producer: Bob Ferguson*

Lonely Comin' Down
Do You Hear the Robins Sing
What Ain't to Be, Just Might Happen
The Bird That Never Flew
Comes and Goes
Washday Blues
When I Sing for Him
He Left Me Love
Oh, He's Everywhere
Still on Your Mind

**My Tennessee Mountain Home**
*RCA APL1-0033*
*Producer: Bob Ferguson*

The Letter
I Remember
Old Black Kettle
Daddy's Working Boots
Dr. Robert F. Thomas
In the Good Old Days (When Times Were Bad)
My Tennessee Mountain Home
The Wrong Direction Home
Back Home

# DOLLY PARTON

The Better Part of Life
Down on Music Row

## Bubbling Over
*RCA APL1-0286*

## Jolene
*RCA APL1-0473*
*Producer: Bob Ferguson*

Jolene
When Someone Wants to Leave
River of Happiness
Early Morning Breeze
Highlight of My Life
I Will Always Love You
Randy
Living on Memories of You
Lonely Comin' Down
It Must Be You

## Love Is Like A Butterfly
*RCA APL1-0712*
*Producer: Bob Ferguson*

Love Is Like a Butterfly
If I Cross Your Mind
My Eyes Can Only See You
Take Me Back
Blackie, Kentucky
Gettin' Happy
You're the One That Taught Me How to Swing
Highway Headin' South
Once Upon a Memory

## The Bargain Store
*RCA APL1-0950*
*Producers: Porter Wagoner and Bob Ferguson*

The Bargain Store
Kentucky Gambler

## DOLLY PARTON

When I'm Gone
The Only Hand You'll Ever Need to Hold
On My Mind Again
I Want to Be What You Need
Love to Remember
You'll Always Be Special to Me
He Would Know
I'll Never Forget

### Dolly (The Seeker/We Used To)
*RCA APL1-1221*
*Producer: Porter Wagoner*

The Seeker
My Heart Started Breaking
Hold Me
I'll Remember You As Mine
Because I Love You
We Used To
The Love I Used to Call Mine
Bobby's Arms
Only the Memory Remains
Most of All Why

### All I Can Do
*RCA APL1-1665*
*Producers: Porter Wagoner and Dolly Parton*

All I Can Do
The Fire That Keeps You Warm
When the Sun Goes Down Tomorrow
I'm a Drifter
Falling Out of Love with Me
Shattered Image
Boulder to Birmingham
Preacher Tom
Life's Like Poetry
Hey, Lucky Lady

# DOLLY PARTON

## New Harvest ... First Gathering
*RCA APL1-2188*
*Producer: Dolly Parton (co-produced with*
*Gregg Perry)*

Light of a Clear Blue Morning
Applejack
My Girl (My Love)
Holdin' onto You
You Are
How Does It Feel
Where Beauty Lives in Memory
(Your Love Has Lifted Me) Higher and Higher
Getting in My Way
There

## Here You Come Again
*RCA APL1-2544*
*Producer: Gary Klein*

Here You Come Again
Baby Come Out Tonight
It's All Wrong, But It's All Right
Me and Little Andy
Lovin' You
Cowgirl and the Dandy
Two Doors Down
God's Coloring Book
As Soon As I Touched Him
Sweet Music Man

## Anthologized Dolly
A listing of RCA country music anthologies that
have included songs by Dolly Parton. Some of
these are cuts from other Parton albums; some of
them—the *Concert* and *Grand Ole Opry* albums—
are live performances.

## DOLLY PARTON

**Award Winners**
*RCA APL1-2262*

I Will Always Love You

**Best of a Great Year, Vol. 3**
*RCA CPL2-0449*

My Tennessee Mountain Home

**The Best of Chet Atkins and Friends**
*RCA APL1-1985*

Do I Ever Cross Your Mind

**50 Years of Country Music**
*Camden ADL2-0782*

**Good Old Country Gospel**
*RCA LSP-4778*

Wings of a Dove

**Great Moments at the Grand Ole Opry**
*RCA CPL2-1904*

Coat of Many Colors

**Stars of the Grand Ole Opry**
*RCA CPL2-0466*

Mule Skinner Blues

**20 Great Country Hits**
*RCA CPL2-1286*

Love Is Like a Butterfly

**In Concert**
*RCA CPL2-1014*

Rollin' in My Sweet Baby's Arms (duet with
Ronnie Millsap)

# DOLLY PARTON

Coat of Many Colors
The Bargain Store
Jolene
Love Is Like a Butterfly

## Singles Dolly
*(A list of 45 RPM singles by Dolly that are still in release by RCA "Dumb Blonde" by Monument):*

The Bargain Store/The Seeker
Coat of Many Colors/Touch Your Woman
Dumb Blonde/Somethin' Fishy
Here You Come Again/Me and Little Andy
I Will Always Love You/Lonely Comin' Down
It's All Wrong, But It's All Right/Two Doors Down
Jolene/My Tennessee Mountain Home
Joshua/Mule Skinner Blues
Just Because I'm a Woman/My Blue Ridge
   Mountain Boy
Light of a Clear Blue Morning/There
Love Is Like a Butterfly/Sacred Memories

## Other Peoples' Dolly
A partial list of some of the more noteworthy recordings of Dolly Parton's songs by other artists:

### The Seeker
Merle Haggard—It's All in the Movies,
*Capitol ST-11483*
*(Dolly plays guitar on this and on Haggard's record of "Kentucky Gambler")*
Danny Davis and the Nashville Brass—
Country Gold
*RCA APL1-1240*

### All I Can Do
Mary Kay Place—Tonight at the Capri Lounge
*Columbia PC-34353*
The Statler Brothers—The Country America Loves,
*Mercury SRM1-1125*

## DOLLY PARTON

### Kentucky Gambler
Merle Haggard—Keep Movin' On
*Capitol ST-11365*
and Songs I'll Always Sing
*Capitol SABB-11531*

### You Are
Andy Williams—Get Together
*Columbia CS-9952*

### Fuel To the Flame
Skeeter Davis—Best of Skeeter Davis
*RCA APL1-0190*

### The Little Things
Bobby Goldsboro—10th Anniversary Album,
*United Artists UA-LA311-H2*
Jerry Reed—Red Hot Picker
*RCA APL-1226*

### Put It Off Until Tomorrow
Loretta Lynn—You Ain't Woman Enough
*MCA 6*
The Osborne Brothers—Ru-be-eee
*MCA 135*

### My Tennessee Mountain Home
Maria Muldaur—Maria Muldaur
*RPS 2148*
Earl Scruggs Revue—Rockin' Across the Country
*Columbia KC-32943*

### Jolene
Olivia Newton-John—Come On Over
*MCA 3016*

### I Will Always Love You
Linda Ronstadt—Prisoner in Disguise
*Asylum 7E1045*
*(Dolly sings backup)*

## DOLLY PARTON

### Coat of Many Colors
Emmylou Harris—Pieces of the Sky
*Reprise 2213*

### To Daddy
Emmylou Harris—
Quarter Moon in a Ten-Cent Town
*Warner Brothers WB 3141*